Praise for *Keeru*

'A slim book with the heft of a family saga, *Keeru* is poignant and engrossing, and masterfully narrated by a richly realized cast of characters whose company you will cherish and miss as soon as you turn the last page.'
Deepa Anappara, author of *Djinn Patrol on the Purple Line*

'The loveliest love story I have read in ages. Fauzia has written a crackling, funny, angry short novel with a very big heart. *Keeru* has been forty years in the making and every single word is worth the wait.'
Mohammed Hanif, author of *A Case of Exploding Mangoes*

'A deeply moving letter to diaspora and belonging, this novella is devoid of nostalgia but full of emotional insight. It tackles thorny themes of migration and discrimination in the intensely humanizing way that is the hallmark of great literature.'
Dur e Aziz Amna, author of *American Fever*

Praise for the author

'Amidst the clutter of mangoes and coconuts that characterizes most diasporic writing, Fauzia Rafique's work is a breath of fresh air as it addresses pertinent social issues beautifully and poignantly.'
Harsha Walia, author of *Border and Rule*

KEERU

Fauzia Rafique is a novelist, poet and an arts organizer. Her Punjabi novel *Keeru* (Lahore, 2019) won Ali Arshad Mir Award 2020 while her debut novel *Skeena* received WIN Canada's Distinguished Novelist & Poet award in 2012. *Skeena*'s Punjabi edition (Lahore, 2007) is Pakistan's most-sold Punjabi novel since 2008. Fauzia's humorous fantasy titled *The Adventures of Saheban: Biography of a Relentless Warrior* was released in 2016. Fauzia's novels have been published in Canada, India and Pakistan. In Pakistan, Fauzia worked as a journalist in the 70s and the 80s. Her adaptation of Dostoevsky's novella became Pakistan Television's first Punjabi drama serial *Appay Ranjha Hoi*.

Haider Shahbaz has a BA from Yale University and is currently doing a PhD in Comparative Literature at UCLA. He is the translator of Mirza Athar Baig's critically acclaimed magnum opus *Hassan's State of Affairs*. He won the 2020 Jawad Memorial Prize for translating Khalida Hussain's short story 'The Sea'. His translations from Urdu have appeared in the *Brooklyn Rail*, *Asymptote*, *Words Without Borders* and elsewhere. He was also the 2016–17 Charles Pick Fellow at the University of East Anglia and was selected as an emerging translator by ALTA (American Literary Translators Association).

Keeru

FAUZIA RAFIQUE

Translated from the Punjabi by
HAIDER SHAHBAZ

hachette
INDIA

First published in Punjabi in 2019 by Sanjh Publications, Lahore
This translation first published in India in 2025 by Hachette India
(Registered name: Hachette Book Publishing India Pvt. Ltd)
An Hachette UK company
www.hachetteindia.com

1

Print ISBN 978-93-5731-934-8
eBook ISBN 978-93-5731-482-4

Hachette Book Publishing India Pvt. Ltd
4th & 5th Floors, Corporate Centre,
Plot No. 94, Sector 44, Gurugram 122003, India

Typeset in Dante MT Std 12/16.5
by R. Ajith Kumar, New Delhi

Printed and bound in India
by Thomson Press India Ltd.

MIX
Paper | Supporting responsible forestry
FSC® C010615

Dedicated to Randeep

کہے حسین سہاگن سائ، جو گل تھیں واہندی نچی

Hussain says, the one who is celebrated is the
one who emerges dancing without a care for convention.

– MADHULAL HUSSAIN

Lahore, 1538–1599

CONTENTS

1

KEERU

My Bebe will be here soon. She will depart from Lahore at half past three today, and after travelling for twenty-four hours, she will arrive at Vancouver Airport at half past four tomorrow. Only thirty hours left before she gets here. I still haven't cleaned the house, bought new bedsheets or found a woman who will take care of her while I'm at work. Parking my car at the warehouse, I started breaking into a cold sweat. So much still needed to be done! I don't care if the whole world hates me as long as my mother loves me. I took out a Tim Hortons napkin from my pocket and wiped my forehead. *Everything will get done in time, don't worry, take a deep breath,* I told myself, and stepped out of the car. My office was right in front of me. Before I entered, I stood outside the door for a moment, trying to envision how it would look to my mother, my Bebe. I noticed, as if for the first time, the black English letters on the cream door:

UNIT 33

HALEEMA BIBI ENTERPRISES LIMITED

Bebe knows a little English. She will recognize her own name instantly, but she might stumble a bit on 'enterprises'. It will fill her with happiness to see her own name on the door. I stepped forward, opened the door and walked into the hall. The wall-to-wall carpet, red and blue, looked clean; the large windows framed the ten women working on sewing machines. I watched the scene as if through a stranger's eyes. I looked to my right – underneath a mop of black hair, wrapped in a blue checkered tank top, two round breasts resting on a white counter – and was suddenly shaken out of my stranger's vision, and now I saw with my own eyes: Aunty Naila, the supervisor of the workroom and my assistant manager.

'Hello, Aunty!' I greeted her loudly, and more warmly than usual, in an attempt to cover up my embarrassment, and then quickly started walking towards my office.

'You got here fifteen minutes early.' Aunty jumped out of her seat and started walking behind me with quick, short steps.

'There's a lot of work today.' I kept walking ahead without meeting her gaze.

A small metal board on my office door: 'Muhammad Hussain Khan Keeru, President'. *Bebe will like it,* I smiled to myself. The window in my office was open. There was a large desk on one side of the window and another smaller desk on the other side. The rest of the room was empty. It was a big office. The previous owner used it to accommodate four managers, as well as an accountant.

'Fifteen people called. I have set up four interviews. After seven today.' Aunty was standing right behind me.

'Only four interviews out of fifteen?'

'The problem is the late hours. Girls don't want to stay the night.'

'Okay, that's fine. I will make sure to get back home by seven.'

'Okay, in that case, we can set the shift from 7 a.m. to 7 p.m.' Aunty turned back towards the workroom.

'Aunty, did you hire someone to clean the house?'

'Yes, it's done. They are the cousins of the same people that clean our office. They just arrived in the country a few months ago – they're a couple. The best rate!'

'When can they do it?'

'Tomorrow morning.'

'Thank you so much. Will you get the bedsheets today?'

'Yes, I need to go to Sears to get some towels. Should I get two sets of queen-sized sheets?'

'Yes, two sets. My mother loves the colour pink, and she likes floral designs.'

'Ah, good you told me; otherwise, I would've gotten the stripes or checkered ones that are more popular these days.' Aunty walked to the door, then turned back to look at me. 'O-ho, I forgot. It's Dasveer's day off today. Who will supervise the workers if I leave?'

'I'll be here. I have to go for a sales meeting around

two, but you will be back by then? What work are they doing today?'

'The same. Hotel uniforms.'

'That's fine. You will be here for the interviews, right?'

'I was going to leave at five-thirty…'

'No, no, Aunty, please, you have to do the interviews with me.' I panicked and stood up from my seat. 'It's not going to work without you. I'll drop you home on my way back.'

'And your uncle's dinner?' Aunty raised her right eyebrow and stared at me.

'Of course, dinner is on me. Uncle loves nihari. We will pick it up from his favourite restaurant on the way back.'

'Okay, I'll head to Sears then.'

Aunty looked pleased with the arrangement. I was satisfied. Everything would happen smoothly as long as Aunty was happy. Today she is my assistant manager, but soon she will be the manager, and then partner. She is capable, and a very nice person too. And I wouldn't be in this position if it wasn't for the kindness of her husband, Uncle Raheem. He gave me my first job in this country, he got me enrolled in a training course for security guards, and he helped me settle down in this city – Surrey. I fiddled with the stationery on my desk. I couldn't focus on work. I was thinking about Bebe.

My Bebe only has two bad habits: She finds whatever meaning she wants to find, no matter what anyone says, and she thinks I'm some kind of genius. I was an ugly, grumpy and mean-spirited child. It's true that I enjoyed reading and writing more than the other kids in our housing colony, but that wasn't because of my superior intellect; it was because of Irfan Sahib. Irfan Sahib was the only son of the school headmaster in our housing colony. He was older and stronger than me, and he loved playing ghoda-ghoda. I used to visit his big house behind the school building. In the middle of their large lounge, I would get on my hands and knees, like a horse, and stare at the floor. I still remember the carpet; it was red. I was too young to wear any shorts or underwear. He used to look at my naked bottom and laugh rowdily before climbing on my back. Then he would say, 'Count after me: One!' and he would strike my ribs with his knees. I would repeat, 'One,' and move forward. Two, three, four… I used to count to fifty, sometimes even more. This is how I learnt to count to a hundred before I even started going to school, and I've never forgotten my lessons. Bebe thinks that I learned all the numbers and ABCs because I am some kind of genius, but… I heard a knock on my door. I sat up straight.

'Come in!'

A young woman, hidden inside a maroon shawl, walked in. She was holding a piece of mustard cotton in her nervous, shaking hands. 'Sir, should there be a buckram in the hem of this apron?'

'Aunty Naila didn't give you a design sheet?' I walked over to Aunty Naila's desk, but I couldn't find the sheet.

'Sorry, sir, it's my first day. I don't understand the sheet.'

'No problem, show me.' I extended my hand, and she extended the cloth towards me. 'No, I mean, show me the sheet.' She ran out of the room. I was already lost in my thoughts again when she came running back. 'Here's the sheet.' She bent forward and handed it to me. I detected a faint scent of henna as I took the sheet from her, and I had this sudden desire to see her henna-filled hands, but I diverted my attention towards the sheet. 'Yes, there should be a buckram.' I put the sheet on the desk, stood up from my seat, and walked to the window.

'Thank you… and sir, please don't tell Aunty.' She grabbed the sheet and quickly left the room.

Don't tell Aunty? Amazing! Who is the boss here! I laughed to myself. *Yes, Aunty should be the boss. Only she can handle this whole mess. I have too many things on my mind.* I returned to my desk and opened the file for the sales meeting on my computer.

Everyone has some fears, some worries, some problems that keep them up at night. I have two that have never left me. I spent my childhood, my teenage years, and now I'm spending my youth under the weight of these two worries. One is my mother, and the other is my name. I could never understand either. I was still quite young when I first heard the meaning of my name. Irfan Sahib's cousins were visiting. All the children – me, Irfan Sahib, his cousins – gathered in the schoolyard after dinner to play chor-police. Some children became policemen, some became judges and some became thieves.

'I'm a policeman,' I declared.

'You?' Irfan Sahib burst out laughing. His cousins followed his lead, like they did in everything else, and started laughing too.

'I know how to shoot a pistol.' I put my right knee on the ground, made a pistol out of my left hand, and held it in my right hand, raised my elbows, and started firing – *tha tha tha*.

'Stop!' Irfan Sahib scolded.

I stopped shooting and looked at him.

'You can't be a policeman.'

'Why?'

'How are you going to be a policeman, motherfucker, when your name is Keeru?'

'So what?' I didn't understand what he was trying to say.

'You don't know what Keeru means? It means you're a lowly insect, a bug, a pest… *vermin*.' He slapped my forehead, and I fell backwards.

'So what can I be?' I started crying.

'You…' He drifted off.

'Look, he's a girl, crying like a little girl!' A boy kicked me in the stomach.

'He's a girl; let's kidnap her.'

They picked me up and started carrying me around the courtyard. The kids who became policemen tried to snatch me away from the others. They grabbed me, clawed at me, kicked me. I fell on the concrete floor many times. I was terrified and started screaming. This spurred them on even more. I felt like my heart would explode from fear. Some adults finally arrived on the scene. Irfan Sahib told his cousins to stop and took them inside the house. Before they left, they all kicked me while I lay curled up on the ground, sobbing. At that moment, I heard the screams of another child. It was Irfan Sahib's younger sister, Dolly Baby. Nobody had paid any attention to my loud screams, but everybody was immediately galvanized at the first sound of Dolly Baby's cries. All the adults appeared instantly. The nanny arrived in a matter of seconds, picked up Dolly Baby in her arms and started rocking her. The cook and the clerk arrived at the scene, abandoning their work, and then returned when they were satisfied that the baby was fine. I remained lying on the floor. I cried even more. Where was my Bebe? My body shook and trembled. I felt the injustice deeply. Someone picked me up. It was the school's new security guard, an Afghan refugee, with a real, genuine gun. Irfan Sahib, and everyone else, feared him.

He pulled me up and helped me stand on my feet. He made me walk a few steps. Then he picked me up and brought me to the door of the inner courtyard. I went up to my Bebe, tears still running down my face. She was sitting in front of the tap outside the kitchen.

'Bebe.' I clung to her back.

'What happened, my life? It's okay, have some patience. Can't you see that I have an expensive plate in my hand?' She jerked her shoulders, and I fell on my back. She had a pile of dirty dishes in front of her. She didn't even turn around to look at me – just continued washing. I lay there, powerless, and kept crying. Once she was finished washing all the dishes, stacking them up in a basket and securing the basket with a cloth, she turned around and picked me up from the floor.

'Come,' she hugged me, 'my beautiful baby.'

My breath finally returned to me.

She took off my shirt, pushed me under the tap and turned it on. The cold water stung my body, but it also soothed me. She wrapped me in her shawl and carried me home. When we were inside, she searched for each scrape and bruise on my body, treated it with mustard oil, dressed me in a fresh shirt, put me down on the bed and lay down next to me.

'Sleep, my life.' She caressed the bump on my forehead.

For the first time in my life, I asked her the question that I am still asking her.

'Bebe, why did you name me Keeru?'

She never fails to give an answer when I ask this question. But each time, the answer is different.

She hugged me tightly and responded, 'Because you are the insect of my belly.'

I wanted to ask more questions, but she started to tickle me. All my questions dissolved into laughter.

The real trouble started a few weeks later when she took me to the mosque because she wanted me to study the Quran with the imam alongside the other children. At night, after finishing all her work, she washed my clothes, and in the morning, she bathed me, dressed me and took me to the market. She bought a packet of rusk biscuits and a small packet of almonds for the imam, and she bought a canvas bag and blue rubber flip-flops for me. After putting on my new flip-flops on my feet and my new bag on my shoulder, I felt like a peacock walking the streets of our town. Both those items were mine, mine from the beginning; they weren't hand-me-downs. Nobody had used them before me. The imam was sitting outside the mosque, under a rosewood tree. People were assembled around him. Some of them had also brought their children to study at the mosque. When our turn came, Bebe offered the rusk biscuits and almonds to the imam, who accepted them after blessing me with a blow of his breath. He instructed his assistant to note down my name. When the assistant asked my mother for my name, she replied, 'Keeru,' and people burst out laughing.

'Father's name?' the assistant asked.

'Muhammad 'Usain.'

'Muhammad Hussain.' The assistant corrected the pronunciation and started writing in his register.

'Don't take the prophet's name in vain!' the imam interjected. 'You cannot mix this name with the holy name of the Prophet Muhammad, peace and salutations be upon him, or the holy name of Imam Hussain, peace be upon him.' Then he asked my mother, 'What is your name? Show me your identity card.'

Bebe showed him her identity card.

'Haleema Alice Bibi? Okay, so you are Christian.' The imam switched from Punjabi to Urdu.

'Yes, but his father was a Muslim.'

'God forgive us all! So there was no legal marriage ceremony? The child is a bastard!'

'No! Why bastard? Of course, we were legally married...'

'How could that be? Have you accepted Islam?'

'Yes, why not! My parents gave me the name Bibi, the priest changed it to Alice Bibi, and the imam who performed my marriage ceremony took out the Alice and changed it to Haleema Bibi. Now this is my name...'

'Bibi, you go back home for now, and come back tomorrow evening, after prayers, and then we will change the boy's name with the will and mercy of God, but we can't do anything before that...'

Tears rushed out of her eyes – the good eye and the bad eye. I got scared and stood up. When Bebe cries from both eyes, it's always the sign of an oncoming tempest. I grabbed and tugged her hand, pulling her upwards. She glanced at me through her tears, stood up and started walking behind me, holding my hand, just like I walked behind her when I cried, holding her hand. In that moment, I was her son and her mother. I liked being able to lead her in this way. I arrived at the school's main gate instead of the back gate that led directly to our home. The security guard opened the little black door, fixed inside the bigger gate, for us to enter.

'Did you enrol him?' the guard asked Bebe.

'They didn't let me enrol him! The imam says we have to change his name first.' She started crying even louder.

'Change the name? What's wrong with his name?'

'He was actually okay with Keeru, but he got stuck on the name of his father, rest in peace, and he says that his name cannot be joined with the names of Muhammad and 'Usain. Now I can't change his father's name, can I? We will have to change his name. Who knows what that imam is going to name my little child!'

'Keeru Khan! Will you change your name?' the guard asked me.

At that time, I, that is, Keeru, was rather content with myself, and I didn't see any reason to change anything, so I shook my head emphatically.

'No? Then how will you go study the Quran at the mosque?'

Bebe began to wail. Baba Khan and I panicked at her despair.

'Listen, sister, this is our Keeru Khan! He is the joy of all our lives!'

'Keeru Khan?' My mother was puzzled.

'You should take Keeru Khan to the other mosque tomorrow and get him enrolled there. Tell them that his father's name was Muhammad Hussain Khan.'

That is how my name changed from Keeru to Keeru Khan.

I still remember Baba Khan – tall, fair, young, handsome; he always wore clean, starched white clothes with a red-and-white turban. He used to pick me up with his two arms as if I was a weightless bird. If anyone ever cared for me, other than my mother, it was Baba Khan. The memories make me sad now. I also remember Saeen Manka, the Saint of Beads, but not as well. Saeen Manka used to wear long, colourful gowns – red and green and orange. He was called the Saint of Beads because, whenever he was displeased or angry, he would snatch at and break the necklace of wood and glass beads around his neck, scattering the beads everywhere. It was said that whoever picked up one of the scattered beads was granted their wish. Bebe once told me that Cheemo's disabled sister's marriage was only arranged due to a bead from Saeen Manka; it would have been impossible otherwise.

Back then, my mother wanted to register my name as

Keeru Hussain, and today, the nameplate hanging outside my office reads 'Muhammad Hussain Khan Keeru'. Here, nobody knows what Keeru means, and even if they do, they cannot say, 'God forgive us all' and humiliate me or threaten to kill me. Keeru is just my poetic pen name now, my takhallus, and sometimes I gather up the courage to write a few verses under this name.

I couldn't concentrate. Only twenty-five hours left until my Bebe arrived. Aunty hadn't returned yet. I would leave once she returned. I wanted to get a coffee and sit somewhere before my meeting, clear my head. I was not too worried about the meeting. I was going to meet some Sikh brothers, not any white people. They ran a company based in Chilliwack, which supplied linens to hotels and hospitals. A few months back, we sent them a quote for a business contract, and even though we didn't get the contract, they set up this meeting. I thought that maybe they wanted to talk about another job. It was almost two now. I collected my things and put them in my briefcase. Aunty was usually on time.

I heard women laughing outside. Aunty must have returned.

'Sir, look at this, I got a fantastic deal! I'm sure it's the blessings of your mother's prayers.' Aunty took out six colourful packages of bedsheets from oversized Sears bags and placed them on the table. 'The floral sheets were 60 per cent off!' She handed one to me.

Pink and dark-red roses blooming next to parrot-green leaves on a white cloth. 'Perfect,' I exclaimed. 'Bebe will love these!'

'Bebe? Sir, you should start saying "Mummy" now.'

Bebe appeared in front of my eyes: a short, scrunched salwar kameez in faded colours; a black shawl covering her head with a corner pulled forward to hide her bad eye; her dark complexion.

'I don't know, Aunty.' I smiled. 'It's not a bad idea.'

I walked out of the office.

The meeting was in a South Asian restaurant on Scott Road. I stopped at a Tim Hortons on the way. The long line of customers stretched all the way outside the coffee shop. I joined the end of the queue. The hours at the office had made me lethargic, and it felt good to stand outside under the warm sunlight, a breeze blowing past me. The weather here is sweet at this time of the year. In Lahore, it gets unbearably hot by May. This is why I booked Bebe's ticket for April. I wanted her to leave Lahore before the height of summer. I don't want her to get a heatstroke in the summer, and when it is winter, I worry that her bones and joints will ache, or her jaw will lock. The line moved, and I entered the coffee shop. Four counters were running; it didn't take me long to get to the front of the line. There was complete mayhem inside the shop. Children were yelling and running around the tables and chairs. Their mothers shouted at them to sit still and then warned them that any child who was running and shouting would not get any treats. The kids stopped – but only for a second. Then they started playing ghoda-ghoda. One of them climbed on the other one's back and straddled him. They were white kids, of course. They could be as noisy as they wanted. No one was going to say anything to them. If they were our kids, someone would've scolded them by now. I used to enjoy playing the part of the horse; besides, Irfan Sahib never let me be the rider. Once I complained, and he started shouting at me, 'You're talking nonsense. You are my horse. I am not your horse.' I objected that it was only a game. 'So what? I can't be your horse.' I asked him why, and he responded with his own question: 'Does my mother work in your house?' I told him that she didn't. 'That's it then.'

I didn't fully understand Irfan Sahib, but I knew at that moment that I didn't want to be around him as much any more. I was growing up. I depended less on Bebe, and I started to spend more time hanging around my street instead of the headmaster's house. One day, Irfan Sahib threw out all his English textbooks in the garbage heap outside. I picked them up, and with some guidance from Baba Khan, I started to recognize the alphabets. Soon, I could read the letters, and even though I still didn't know how to join them, I liked sitting on the steps outside our door and reciting the alphabets to myself. The other children used to watch me and feel jealous. Someone's uncle had performed the Hajj, someone's father owned a corner store, someone's mother returned from the office in a tonga – all the children wore new clothes on Eid. Everyone had someone. Bebe and I were on our own. I did not have anything except those English textbooks. Once, I was sitting on the steps and reciting the alphabet when Chunnu, his snot sliding all the way down to his upper lip, walked up and sat next to me on the steps. He asked, 'What's written in the book?' 'Wipe your nose first,' I ordered dismissively. He quickly put his torn sleeve underneath his nose and gave it a few hard rubs. I started making up a story, loosely following the illustrations in the textbook. 'Where did you get this book?' Chunnu stared at the pages with his gunk-crusted eyes. 'It's come from *foreign*.' I closed the book and put my hand over it. Chunnu continued his interrogation: 'Where did you get it? From Irfan Sahib? He is your friend?' I nodded. 'Like Sheeda is my friend?' I didn't respond to his question directly. 'We play ghoda-ghoda.' 'Us too!' He shouted, jumped off the steps onto the street and bent over like a horse. 'Come, I'll be the horse first.' I kept sitting. Chunnu's mother doesn't work at my house. So then?

Eventually, I did understand what Irfan Sahib was trying to say – it took me a long time, but I got it. But something I've never understood to this day is why, a few years after this little conversation, Chunnu, following Irfan Sahib and the others, stood in that same spot and falsely accused me of blasphemy against the Prophet Muhammad.

Leave this topic alone, I softly told my heart. *Think of the meeting. Think of Bebe. She will be here soon.* My body shook from inside, and for a split second, I felt like I was going to fall to the ground, but I kept standing. *It's all right. Everything is all right. You will keep standing right here.* I took deep, long breaths until I felt stable.

The woman in front of me in the queue was now at the counter. I started rehearsing my order in my head.

'Hello!' The white woman at the counter greeted me.

'Coffee to go, black, medium,' I told her.

'Is that all?'

'Yes, please, thank you.'

I tapped my card and stepped aside to wait for my coffee. The bedsheets were pretty; they would look nice with the silver-grey carpet. As I picked up my coffee, I remembered that the blinds in Bebe's room at my place were black. In Pakistan, we used to have a tiny stove inside our one-room home; the smoke blackened all the walls. Bebe had to whitewash them every month. I called Aunty, but her cell phone was busy. When I got into the car with my coffee, Aunty called back.

'Aunty, I need to change the black blinds in Bebe's room.'

'Yes, of course, no problem.' She took a short, sharp breath and then said, 'I have a curtain set lying around at home, cotton satin, pink and green colours; the size will fit, I think. You can check it, too. I will remember to give it to you at night when you drop me back. The cleaners will come in the morning and hang it up.'

Aunty is Aladdin's genie, I thought. *What is your command? She will fulfil it before you finish saying it.* I started the car, smiling to myself. Today's meeting was just a casual get-together, but I was still feeling a little disoriented. *Should I postpone it to next week? There's only fifteen minutes left before the meeting, Scott Road is right around the corner, just take a bitter sip of the coffee and get going.* I drove out of the parking lot.

It took me less than ten minutes to arrive at the meeting place. It used to be an Indian sweet shop, but now they've opened a whole restaurant next to it. I looked in front of me as I parked the car – a beautiful, young man stared back at me with his big, sweet eyes. When I parked the car and stepped outside, he came over, smiling.

'Muhammad Hussain Keeru?' He extended his hand.

'Haan ji.' The Punjabi words escaped my mouth. I gripped his hand with both my hands.

'Daljeet Singh.' He smiled wide enough to flash his front teeth, which made him look even more endearing.

'Oh, okay, so you're Daljeet…'

'Yes, it's me. And I recognized you! I got a chance to hear you recite your poem at the last Punjabi Writers' Gathering. It was brilliant.'

I followed him inside the restaurant. 'You are a member of the Writers' Gathering too?'

'No, I live in Chilliwack. I was just visiting with my cousin.'

'Okay, but why don't I remember you from the meeting? Your face is very memorable…'

He laughed. 'There were lots of artists and writers visiting from Punjab. The room was full.'

We sat down.

'I still remember two lines from your poem: "Breath thumps with your thoughts for years and decades."'

'You must've heard my poem, "Kaal: Dearth."'

'I don't remember the entire poem now, but I do remember listening to it.'

'Thank you so much.' My heart was beating a little faster. 'You are a poet too?'

'No, not at all. But I like to sing.'

'Oh, amazing! Where can I hear you sing? You must play some instrument too?'

'Guitar, a little…'

By the time we finished our lunch, it was already five. I didn't even notice the time. Daljeet and I shared the same ideas with regards to business – we both wanted to create a retail sales network in addition to tenders and wholesale contracts. I told him about the small business network we had tried to launch six months ago, but neither me nor Aunty had been able to focus on it properly. He assured me, 'We will do it together.' I felt encouraged. Most of Daljeet's family – his parents and two younger sisters – still lived in Chandigarh. He lived in Chilliwack with his elder sister and brother-in-law. The brother-in-law owned the business. It was doing well; they had a few good contracts. Daljeet wanted to start a business of his own, something that would complement his brother-in-law's business while also giving him the opportunity to own his own business and bring his family over here. We decided to meet again soon. Daljeet was spending the weekend here. I invited him to my place for dinner on Friday, and he agreed. I texted him my address right then and there.

'My Be— my Mummy is coming tomorrow from Lahore.' I picked a round gulab jamun from the bowl in front of me, held up the dripping, syrupy ball of dough in front of him and then popped the whole thing in my mouth.

Daljeet smiled at me, then picked up the remaining two balls of gulab jamuns and put them both in his mouth. He looked funny with his round, inflated cheeks. I started laughing, and seeing me, he also started laughing. We barely managed to swallow our gulab jamuns.

'I call her Bebe, my Mummy. I told you about Aunty Naila, our assistant manager. She told me that I should say Mummy instead of Bebe, but it feels strange to me. What do you say?'

'Bee-Ji. From BiBi Ji.'

'From Bibi Ji to Bee-Ji, so from Bebe Ji to Be-Ji...' I caught myself thinking out loud.

'Okay, so it's a "Welcome to Canada" party for Be-Ji on Friday.' Daljeet raised both his hands upward and outward like he was about to break into a bhangra dance move.

'Yes,' I shouted. His enthusiasm was infectious, and I suddenly felt like a weight had lifted from my shoulders, even though I had only been thinking of a meeting, not a party.

'I will be there at seven.' Daljeet got up.

'The bill...' I turned towards the counter.

'Don't worry, the bill will go to the company.' He stood at the door, holding it open. 'It's my cousin's restaurant.'

On the way back, I was lost in thought again. Why didn't I think of a party? Parties happen where there is family, where there are friends. What was my party? Taking ten cans of beer to Uncle Raheem's place and sitting with him all evening, listening to his boring stories about his boring life. Occasionally, I go to gatherings of Urdu and Punjabi writers, and my heart feels lighter for a while, but sometimes, even these meetings make me feel alien, out of place. I get up, leave, go somewhere else.

Aunty conducted four interviews in the evening. I just sat there silently, playing the role of the boss. One of the interviewees was quite old herself, one couldn't drive, one looked too sharp, like she could hustle Bebe or insult her.

The fourth had such a sad face – Bebe would get depressed just looking at her. Nothing worked.

'Sir, there's one more candidate; she couldn't come today. Should I set an interview for the day after tomorrow?'

'Day after tomorrow I will be home. Be... Be-Ji... Bebe will be here. Can she come to the house?'

'This girl lives close to your place, speaks Urdu-Hindi, has a driving license, and she was born and raised here, so she can do any chores outside the house. She says her cooking is "not good", but that's okay, Mummy-ji can train her to cook the way she likes her food.'

'Sounds good. Schedule it for 2 p.m., day after tomorrow.'

We locked the unit and walked out. Aunty sat in the front seat next to me. Her warmth filled the front of the car. It felt like she was both near me and far from me.

'Your uncle likes Pakwan's nihari these days, but we will have to go further up for it. Let's just get it from Al-Medina.'

'Sure? Pakwan is only fifteen–twenty minutes more.'

'Right now, every minute is too much. I left the house at six in the morning; it's nine now.'

'Sounds good.' I directed the car towards Scott Road Station. 'Do you want to order on the phone? It'll save some time.' I could tell from Aunty's tone that she was exasperated; it was best to distract her with some tasks right now.

'What should I order?' She started dialling.

'Nihari, roti and salad.'

'One nihari?' Her tone was still irritable.

'Four…'

'Four?'

I was watching the road, but I could tell that Aunty was asking the question with her right eyebrow raised in a perfect arch.

'Yes,' I responded. 'Two for you, two for me. I'll keep one for Bebe's breakfast when she arrives.'

'One is enough for us. It's too heavy; I can never finish it.'

'Get a chicken karahi in that case.'

'I feel like a lamb pulao, with raita.'

'Absolutely, get it.'

'Three niharis, six rotis, one lamb pulao, one raita,' Aunty ordered.

'And four ras malais.' Aunty loves ras malai for dessert.

'Sir, today you are really…'

I didn't bother to hear what she said next. Once she called me 'sir', I knew that her mood was improving. After placing the order, she called Uncle and started talking to him. When we arrived, I parked the car and went inside to pick up the order. She is not old; I call her Aunty because she is married to Uncle. But otherwise, she looks girlish – young, thin, smart. They don't have any children. People think we are husband and wife when they see us together.

I would be so lucky to have a wife like her.

'Your Uncle says we must host a dinner at our place for Mummy-Ji on Friday. He says he will do the barbecue himself.' Aunty started talking as soon as I got back in the car.

'Okay.' I was not really listening as I handed her the food.

'Remember how much your Uncle liked to barbecue? He used to barbecue every day; now, only here and there.' She stopped talking.

The air inside the car got heavier. I remembered it like yesterday, both of them laughing together, living their happy lives. The accident turned him into a bitter person and her into a workaholic. He couldn't leave the bed for the first year. Now he can walk with crutches but still hasn't tried to find any work. Aunty works full-time and then goes home to prepare food for dinner and the next day's lunch. When she can't cook herself, she brings food from outside. Uncle sits in front of the TV, reads newspapers.

'What else does Mummy-Ji like to eat? Any vegetable? Dessert? I will prepare it tomorrow and leave it for her.'

'Oh! I forgot. You must come to my place on Friday. There's a party.'

'Party? At your place?' She raised her eyebrow again. 'Who else is coming?'

'Just you two, me… and one or two friends.'

'What friends?'

'You will meet them at the party.'

I sat in the car for a few minutes in front of their townhouse. Aunty went inside to get the curtains, then handed me the packet, and I left.

When I got home, I showered and then dug into the nihari until my belly was ready to burst. Afterwards, I put the coffee on, picked up the curtains Aunty had given me and went to Bebe's apartment. My house has three portions – one upstairs, which has four bedrooms, and two downstairs. The upper portion is rented by four geologists, who have come from other Canadian provinces for work contracts here in British Columbia. Once their contract ends, they come and rest here before they get another contract. I have never had any problems with them. The portion downstairs with two bedrooms is mine; the other one, which has a single bedroom, will be Bebe's. I was living in the latter portion until March while both the other portions were rented out. Then I asked the tenants to leave the two-bedroom portion, moved there myself and prepared the one-bedroom portion for Bebe. The only problem is that there is no door between my portion and Bebe's portion; you have to first go outside, though both entrances are in the same veranda. Both have doors that open into the house's lobby, which also leads to the upstairs portion. I thought about asking the geologists to leave, so I could move upstairs with Bebe and rent the two portions downstairs, but it won't work. The rent from the upper portion pays the mortgage; the combined rent from both the downstairs portions would still be less than upstairs since they are in the basement.

I had applied my own colour scheme in Bebe's apartment – two black walls, two silver-grey walls and black blinds. I removed the blinds. It was pitch-black outside. I watched the darkness. I felt like I had seen this very darkness before. Then I remembered the time when Bebe and I had built a window in our one-room home. I smiled to myself; my Bebe is a strange one. I must have been five or six years old. I had just returned home from reading stories to Chunnu. Bebe grabbed me affectionately and said, 'Let's play a game.' She stacked the bed vertically against the wall, took off her shawl and told me, 'I'm going to climb up and take out a brick from the wall, hide it in my shawl, then send it down to you. You have to check if there is a brick in the shawl or not. If there is a brick, you take it out of the shawl and stack it by that wall.' She pointed to the opposite wall. Then she said, 'You are still small; I'm not sure if you can handle the brick.' I replied, 'Bebe, I can pick up the brick with one hand!' She said, 'I will end the game if you pick it up with one hand. The brick must be picked up with both hands in this game.' I nodded, and we began to play. Bebe climbed on the bed with a trowel in her hand. I stood on the ground, waiting. She loosened one brick after another, wrapped it in her shawl and lowered it towards me. I would wait for the shawl to drop to the ground, then search for the brick. Once I found it, I would pick it up with both hands and stack it by the wall. As soon as I would stack it, Bebe would clap her hands and shout, 'Keeru is a lion, my hero!' My chest would rise, and I would flash her a proud smile. By the time we made a sizeable hole in the wall, we began to feel tired. She stepped down, pulled the bed away from the wall, picked me up and showed me the outside through the window. Pitch-black. I was mesmerized and couldn't look away. She placed a sweet bread in my hand. Stars began to appear in the dark sky outside. A light breeze started. We both looked out into the darkness and ate our bread.

Coffee must have been done a while back. I picked up the blinds, turned off the lights, locked the apartment, stored the blinds behind the little corner table in the veranda, and went back to my apartment. I poured the coffee in my cup, put on a *tha-tha* gringo action film and sat in front of the TV.

I got stuck in traffic and arrived later than I planned, but I was still standing in the arrivals lounge before the plane landed. All around me, there was hustle and bustle, women and children, Sikhs and Christians and Muslims, Black and white and brown… everyone waiting for their loved ones. Today, my wait would end; my eyes started to tear up. Seventeen years; twelve months in each year;

thirty days in each month; twenty-four hours in each... *Oho, pay attention, man, be careful; don't let your tears ruin Bebe's new coat.* I moved the coat's arm away from my face and took out a tissue from my pocket to wipe my face. *Pay attention, this tissue is the same one from the morning, all used and crumpled.* I dropped it back in my pocket and wiped my face with the back of my right hand. I had ordered Bebe's coat online; it must've been two months ago. I had to search a lot on Google to find the perfect coat. First, I searched for 'ladies coat', but it kept showing me white people's slim-fit fashion; I searched for 'old ladies coat', then I found something useful: ankle-length, real wool, feather-light, $399. I have never bought such expensive clothes. I usually go to Value Village once or twice a year and buy a trunk full of first-class suits, shoes, ties, T-shirts, jeans, everything. But I promised myself I would not get anything second-hand for my mother. I don't remember her ever wearing new clothes. Once, she got a new cloth on Christmas – real elegant, silk, pink with blue flowers on it. I felt it, smelled it. She said, 'Keeru, don't touch it with your dirty hands, I'm going to exchange it with the schoolteacher.' I told her, 'Bebe, you should wear it yourself; it's yours,' but she said, 'I don't like it. It's too flashy, the cloth is too swishy.' I thought she would exchange it with the schoolteacher and get some new cloth that she likes, but when she came back, huffing and puffing, she was carrying a bag of wheat flour, a packet of cane sugar and a tin of oil. She put the stuff down and declared, 'We will make sweet roti and eat it all winter!' And we did. The whole winter, we were full, eating roti and sweet roti.

People were coming out of arrivals now. I stood straight, alert, waiting. Everybody kept passing me. Bebe must have a lot of luggage; she must be collecting it from the belt. How will she carry and drag all the luggage herself? I kept looking, waiting. What does Bebe look like now? She used to wear her black shawl all the time. I was getting tired of looking through the glass wall at the lobby inside when I finally spotted her. Lavender salwar-kameez, lavender shawl with white embroidery, a bright Christian rosary around her neck, black pump shoes, she was pushing her cart with another brown Muslim tasbih in her hand. Bebe! My heart was happy!

One thing was the same as before: a corner of the shawl draped over her left eye.

I stepped forward and hugged her. She kept looking at me, blessing me, crying inconsolably. I was no better.

'Bebe, let's go home.' I held Bebe with one hand, took the cart with the other hand and started walking.

Life is perfect, I thought.

'Oh, Keeru, look, son, there are so many Sikhs here wearing their turbans.' Bebe stopped and observed.

'Yes, Bebe, this isn't Pakistan.'

'Over there, you can't see a Sikh turban outside Punja

Sahib. Since you've moved here, I'm even afraid to get dressed and go to the church alone on Christmas.'

'Bebe, when you walk out of our house here and get to the main road, the church is right there, across the road. You can go every day, definitely on Sundays.'

'Mashallah. And where is the gurdwara?'

'Three or four blocks, that's it.'

'Mosque?'

'That's the closest one,' I laughed. 'You don't even have to cross the main road to get there.'

When we were about to exit the arrivals lounge, I told her to stop and handed her the coat. 'Bebe, it's a little cold outside, wear this.'

'It's so soft and light like a feather.' She caressed the coat all over. 'May you live a long life, my son. It looks very expensive.'

'Thank you, Bebe.' I felt proud. 'Twelfth May was Mother's Day. I got it then and kept it as a present for you.'

'Keep living. May you live a long and happy life.' She missed a step while blessing me.

'Bebe?'

'It's okay. Doctor gave me some medicine for nausea; he told me I'll sleep the whole way, I won't even feel the travel. It really knocked me out. My brain feels squishy, and my body is still swaying from inside.'

Bebe's eyes opened wide when we stepped outside. The sweet sea breeze hit us. She said, 'Child, this is a whole different world!' She was very happy to see the car. I helped her get inside and buckled her seat belt.

I got out of the parking lot. The car was on the road. My world had changed completely.

'Look, Bebe, this is one of the biggest hotels here,' I pointed.

Bebe didn't respond. I looked at her. She was fast asleep. What a character!

I crossed Scott Road and took 72nd Avenue. Bebe woke up. I showed her the church on the right, and the mosque in the corner of the road across from it.

'Very beautiful mosque,' Bebe commented.

I told her that in the year 2000, someone set fire to the mosque and destroyed it, a 'hate crime'; they never found out who did it. This is a new building.

When we got home, I took her straight to her apartment. She said, 'I'm feeling dryness. Warm up some milk for me and crunch a couple of rusk biscuits in it.' Thankfully, I had already gotten some rusk biscuits. I put the milk on the stove and opened the packet of rusk biscuits. Bebe sat on the chair and kept yawning. When she finished her milk and biscuits, I took her to her bedroom. I laid her down and covered her with a blanket. She was asleep before I could walk out. I was going to turn off the light, but then I thought, it's a new place for her, it might get too dark. I turned on a dimmer light, turned off the overhead light, and left.

I couldn't sit still in my apartment. *New place, jet lag. What if she wakes up and starts to panic? I should've kept her in my apartment tonight. What can be done now? Maybe I will watch TV and then go to her apartment and sleep there.*

I felt disoriented. Seventeen years is a lifetime, and on top of that, I was only fourteen when I was separated from Bebe. And the circumstances – I was afraid for my life and worried about her. I didn't feel calm until she moved from that housing colony in Lahore to a village in Multan.

All this happened in 2006. I ran away to save my life. I was bruised everywhere, my head split open; I could feel thick, sticky blood coating my mouth and eyes. That was the second time Baba Khan saved my life. He came running, fired his gun in the air. Everyone fled the scene. He picked me up and took me to the clinic. He got me bandaged. He stayed with me.

I don't know if it was day or night when Bebe arrived, but I remember the delicious broth she kept feeding me. She told me, 'We can't do anything here. Go to Karachi, and from there, get out of this country. Father Francis has given me a name and address. There is some organization; they will apply for you to become a refugee. When you get there, you can bring me there too.' I said to her, 'Come with me, we will both go together.' She started thinking. Then she said, 'May we live long, Keeru, but we don't even have a stalk of husk in our name. Today, your life was threatened, and two sweethearts came to help us, but nobody is going to ask about us tomorrow. Say we both go to Karachi, we don't find any work, we can't even survive two days. I have this job, two thousand rupees guaranteed, my food and shelter are free. While you look for a job, I will send you this money, so you are not looking for a meal and you can put your heart into your work. You have a sharp mind, you understand everything. Focus on the future, don't worry about the past.' Baba Khan spoke plainly; he said, 'Keeru Khan, there's no use going to the police. These jihadi people will kill you even in police custody. Save your life, get on a train to Karachi today.'

When I got to Karachi, I was thankful that Bebe hadn't come with me. Lost on the streets of Karachi, walking aimlessly, trying to find work in factories, getting pushed around, working on daily labour wages. But I never stopped thinking about Bebe and how she was doing. I didn't know if I would ever get to see her again. Our lives had been turned upside down.

And what had happened? It was the month of Ramzan, it was summer. Some of the boys at school surrounded one of our Christian class fellows because he was drinking water during the lunch break. They beat him up until he started bleeding. The headmaster had to come and save him. Irfan Sahib was at the front of the mob that was beating the student, even though he wasn't a student at the school any more – he was a student at Islamia College in Lahore. His father, who was the headmaster, rebuked him in front of everyone. When we got back to class, everyone was still discussing the incident. I said, 'Everyone doesn't have to fast just because Muslims are fasting during Ramzan, everyone has their own fasting rituals. We have Christians, Hindus and Sikhs in our school. This terrible incident shouldn't have happened, and if it has happened, we should call the police and start a proper investigation.' The teacher appreciated my point but quickly ended the discussion right there. That day, after evening prayers, when people had broken their fasts, some ten students from the school, including Irfan Sahib, arrived at my house. I came outside. Irfan Sahib started speaking in a loud, clear voice. I remember his words even today. I don't think I will ever forget them. They echo in my mind.

'You are a street sweeper, an untouchable, musalli, bastard, motherfucker. How dare you say anything against us? You want to call the police on the guardians of Islam? You are only a Muslim on the outside. Inside, you are still Christian. This is blasphemy!'

Everyone started shouting: 'Blasphemy! Blasphemy!'

After that, I only remember two things: extreme fear and extreme pain.

My refugee application took ten months. Bebe sent me money for the first four months. That's how I survived. Then I found some work and told Bebe to stop sending money. A whole new story started when I got to Canada.

I like this story more. I bought a house, Bebe is here now, my business is running smoothly. Meeting Daljeet today gave me even more hope. I think the business will get bigger. We will not want for anything.

I don't think it will take long for Daljeet to establish himself here. His brother-in-law runs a successful business. His uncles live here in Surrey and operate a catering business. And if you want to do any business in Surrey, you can't do it without some support of the Sikh community. Pakistanis are few and far between in this city. It will be really helpful to work with Daljeet because we can build a connection with the Sikh community with his help.

Business meetings only last for half an hour, at most, an hour. But I didn't even feel the time passing when I met Daljeet yesterday. He is full of energy, the kind of person who is the life of the party, who finds something fun in everything around him. I think he really liked my poem, 'Kaal'. He told me to read it for him. I wanted to read it, but then I thought, *This is the problem with poets, wherever they are, they turn the place into a poetry reading.* I would've read it if he was a poet too. He is a singer. I couldn't request him to sing in the middle of the restaurant. I will read my poetry at the party. Hopefully, he will sing there too. His family back home is doing well – a piece of agricultural land, their own house. We have nothing back in Pakistan. He did his B.A.; I never even finished high school. He is good-looking, handsome; I have a plain face. He has an olive complexion; I am dark.

Still, I felt like I had found a companion. I smiled to myself.

It's easier to appreciate yourself and your work when you have someone else who appreciates it too.

After many months, I picked up a paper and started writing a new poem.

I titled it 'Haal: Ecstasy'.

2

HALEEMA

Terrible nightmares, shouts, yells, people scrambling and falling over each other, women screaming. I opened my eyes and sat up.

I saw a wall in front of me, clean like glass, not a single smudge of smoke or dirt. A fan on the ceiling that looked like an expensive toy; the windows covered with pink floral curtains. I could hear birds chirping outside. Could this be paradise? I got out of bed.

I drew open the curtains. They were made of heavy cotton satin; the fabric was brand new. Outside, under the blue sky, a row of tall trees, a wooden fence, a small lawn covered with green grass and flowerbeds full of colourful flowers. This was a well-off person's house.

The room had a single door. I opened it and entered a beautiful drawing room, and on the other side of the room, there was a kitchen, a dining table and four chairs. There was another door in this room. It led to a Western-style bathroom. And across the room, there was a huge window covered with blue curtains. Through a slit in the curtains, I could see large blue flowers. No one was around. Not a human being in sight. Complete and utter silence.

Am I alone? My heart sank.

At that exact moment, the door opened, and a young man with a familiar face, wearing a suit, a red box in his hand, walked in.

'Good afternoon, Bebe!'

'Oh, my love, keep living.' I hugged him. 'It's my Keeru, my heart.'

We both cried in each other's arms.

'Good that you are awake now.' He took me to the sofa and sat me down. 'I was going to wake you up. A girl is coming over. We are going to interview her.'

'A girl, for me?'

'Yes, she will cook for you, take you shopping, drive you around. She'll stay with you from seven in the morning to seven in the evening.'

'How much will you pay her?'

'Eight hundred, cash.'

'Dollars?'

'Yes.'

My heart sank again. Did I come here to burn my son's hard-earned money?

'My life, am I disabled, or am I a child? Tell her not to come; we are not hiring.'

'Bebe, I worry about you being all alone during the day.'

'Why do I need a nanny? I am healthy; my hands and feet still work.'

'Then what should we do? I am out of the house all day. You will get bored or depressed in here.'

'Why? I will have work to do.'

'Work?' He picked a laddu from the red box and took a bite. 'Bebe, taste this, it's delicious.' He handed me the box.

'There are always a hundred things to do in the house. I will find something to work on. What is this black-brown thing?'

'Chocolate.'

'Give me the other one. Yes, that one.'

'Maple, it tastes like honey.'

When I took a bite, I realized it was not a laddu. 'What is this?'

'Doughnut.'

'It's tasty,' I said. Then I continued, 'My son, just listen to this one thing I have to say, and may God listen to everything you say.'

'Bebe, you give the order,' he replied. 'I want you to be happy no matter what.'

'My life, I spent my whole life listening to other people. Do this, sit there, stand here, leave this, pick that, you are a Muslim, you are a Christian, you are this and that. I had no say in my own life. Whatever is left of my life, it starts today. This is my darling God's blessing and the result of your wisdom. Now if you want me to be happy, don't order me around, don't tell me what to do. And if your hand is now full because of God's generosity and your hard work, don't embarrass me about money.'

'O-okay, Bebe. You tell me, how should we do it?'

'What are your monthly expenses for food?'

'About fifteen hundred.'

'For one person?'

'I eat outside. Even if I'm at home, I get food from outside.'

'You hand me the fifteen hundred, I will handle the food expenses. We are not hiring a girl, no nanny or cook.'

'Okay.' He took some money out of his wallet and handed it to me. 'Keep this five hundred. On Tuesday, before going to work, I will take you to the bank; we will open an account for you, and I will deposit fifteen hundred in your account on the first of every month. You will never have to ask me for money. We will see how it works for a couple of weeks. If you don't think the money's enough, I will deposit a larger sum every month. Just don't worry about anything at all.'

'Keep living, my son. May you get whatever your heart desires.' I started to feel better.

He showed me the rest of the house, and he told me that my window opened onto the backyard and his window opened onto the front yard. *Back-yard* and *front-yard*. When I hesitated, he encouraged me and said, 'You know these three words.' He was right; I know front, back and yard. I will learn to combine them soon. My son's house is stunning – a big, roomy backyard, a covered veranda, a door to my apartment on one side and a door to his apartment on the other side, a round table and two chairs in the middle. Flowerpots and flowerbeds all over the yard and veranda. It looked beautiful, mashallah. My son's hard work and my God's blessings. May he live a long life, may he stay protected from the evil eye.

The air travel had shaken my structure – both body and mind. I sat down on the chair in the veranda. Sleep started to catch up with me. I rested my head on the chair – not a worry to bother me – and relaxed. In my dream, I saw a fairy, a girl; she looked like a film star. She was wearing a turquoise silk skirt and tight black bottoms; golden stripes ran through her black hair; a turquoise dot on her forehead; doe-eyed, dark kajal, turquoise glitter on the eyelids; a beaded necklace; earrings as long as her neck; rings and bangles everywhere.

When I opened my eyes, the same girl was standing in front of me. Startled, I stood up.

'Bebe, this is Isabella,' Keeru told me.

'Hello, namaste, salaam.' The girl extended her hand for a handshake.

'Hello.' I shook her hand. It was cold as ice. *Is there any blood in her veins?* 'Take a seat,' I told her.

'Thank you.' She sat. 'Can I call you Bebe?' She spoke

clearly in Urdu, but it sounded like she was speaking English.

'Yes, yes,' I said and then continued in English, 'What your name?'

'Isabella Sarasvati Brown. Bella for short. My mother is Indian, my father, British.'

Keeru left us to speak with each other, and within a few minutes, I could smell something delicious being prepared in the other room. I shouted, 'What are you cooking, Keeru?' He replied, 'Bebe, I am warming some nihari. Come and eat it; bring Bella with you.' When we entered the room, I saw the table, perfectly set up for us to sit down and eat; expensive fine china dinnerware and cutlery, nihari in a covered serving dish, warm roti wrapped in a white cloth, and in a small glass bowl, finely cut onions, tomatoes and slices of lemon. Everything my son does, he does elegantly. May he live a long life.

I was feeling hungry. I put some nihari on my plate, squeezed some lemon on top of it and started eating. Keeru took out two bowls of ras malai from the fridge; he put one in front of me, one in front of Bella. Then he told me that he was going to go visit his workplace. I asked him if he was going to eat before leaving, but he said that he had already eaten three doughnuts. I told him, 'Go safely, take good care. I will finish eating and go to sleep.'

Bella kept sitting with me. She ate the ras malai but didn't even touch the nihari. She said, 'I am not religious, but I still don't eat beef. I can eat chicken.' I asked, 'Do you eat pork?' She said yes. I laughed and told her, 'I am Christian; eating pork is not prohibited for us, but I have lived with Muslims all my life, and it is impossible for me to put it in my mouth.'

She also laughed, then asked me, 'Are you going to interview me now?' I told her, 'Dear daughter, there is no job. My son put up an advertisement by mistake, please forgive us.' She instantly shouted, 'Okay!' and abruptly stood up. I asked her, 'Is everything okay? What happened?' She just kept repeating, 'Thank god, thank god.' Then she took my hand in her ice-cold hands. She said, 'Mummy, I can't do anything.' I said, 'Dear blessed one, why?' She said, 'I'm depressed. I can't get up in the morning, get out of bed, leave the house. It all scares me.' Her eyes started watering and then she started weeping.

I gave her some water and asked her to sit on the sofa with me.

Depression is a tough and awful sickness. When they accused Keeru of blasphemy, they beat him right in the street outside our house. I was out of the colony at the time; I had left for work, and when I returned, I didn't find my son. Bricks, stones, pots, pans, everything was scattered in front of our home. My son's blood hadn't dried yet. I wiped it with my own clothes.

I heard the wife of our neighbour. 'Baba Khan took your son with him. He was firing his gun. He's going to die too now, godforsaken Afghan refugees.' I asked, 'Why did he take Keeru away?' Then she told me that my son had committed blasphemy. I fell on the street and fainted right there. Saeen Manka saw me later, picked me up and took me to the clinic. My son was unconscious, blood-soaked bandages everywhere. *You cruel people! This is an innocent child!* Once he left for Karachi, I fell on the bed and couldn't get up. I couldn't eat or drink, stand or sleep. And most importantly, I had no desire to live or die.

Why did this little young girl get this sickness? I rubbed her hands with mine to make them warmer. She said, 'You are showing me love. When you find out what I have done, you will hate me, but I don't care; it's not like you even have a job.' I said, 'That's undoubtedly true.' She said, 'It's my second month on the street.' I didn't understand what she meant, so she explained that she didn't have a home. She ran away from her home in April; first, she stayed at some hostel, then at a friend's place, then somewhere else and somewhere else.

I remembered running away from my aunt's home. It was very difficult. I was fourteen, I had never left the village, I had no idea where I was going to turn. I was hungry, barefoot. By the time I reached the forest at the edge of our village, it was evening. *God, what should I do now?* There were short, little trees all around me. When it got dark, I climbed a tree and settled in it. I don't remember much, but I remember the unbearable pain in my feet, and on top of it all, I shivered with fear all night. In the morning, I climbed down and started walking again. I walked and walked until the forest ended and I saw a road. I walked alongside it. Then a man saw me walking alone and started following me. I got scared and started running at full speed; he still followed me, running after me. I knew my life was in danger, so I ran and ran. It was God's mercy, I saw a big house in front of me, I pushed the gate, it opened. There was a garden inside; I hid myself. The man didn't enter after me. Then I lost consciousness. Bless Sister Mary. She came there to perform some chore and saw me lying there. It must have taken me a month to get on my feet again. I was bedridden, my feet were wounded, and my insides had dried up from hunger and malnutrition. I couldn't digest anything.

'I'm also a thief.' Bella banged her hand on the arm of the sofa, and I suddenly returned to the scene in front of me. Then she jumped up from the sofa. 'This dress, I stole this dress from Surrey Centre…' and then she kept going and I stole these earrings from there, rings from there., One by one, she pointed at everything she was wearing and told me where she had stolen them from.

'Okay, my girl, you've put together thekriyan to make a waterpot.' I told her the Punjabi proverb. Then she started asking me, 'What do you mean by thekriyan?' I thought hard but couldn't figure out how to explain it to her. Finally, I told her, 'When a clay waterpot breaks, you call the pieces thekriyan.' She started thinking; I could tell she was really trying to figure something out, then she sat down and asked, 'What do you mean by that?' I said, 'You think about the meaning yourself. I am feeling sleepy, I'm going to go lie down.' She said, 'Okay, I will leave.' I asked, 'Where will you go?' She replied, 'I'll go stay with my friend, where I am living these days. It's going to be the first of the month next week; they're going to ask me about money, which I don't have.' I said, 'Dear daughter, if they hassle you, pick up your stuff and come here. You see that sofa? You can sleep on it.' She stared at me with a confused expression. Then she said, 'I thought I was crazy, but you're the crazy one,' and then left.

Her parents have a house here in Surrey, but her father left them a while ago; it's just her mother and two elder sisters now. She said that they always treated her differently from the beginning. The two elder sisters looked like their father – white – but she looked like her mother – dark. The whole family called her stupid and useless. They abused her, blamed her, insulted her, even beat her, and she said, 'One day, I was going to call the police on them.'

'On your own mother and sisters?'

Maybe the police respond to these kinds of calls here. Over there, they don't usually come when people like us call them. And sometimes, they come only to save the murderers, not the weak, the women. This is what happens in blasphemy cases. That's why Baba Khan, Saeen Manka, and Father Francis – all three of them – advised me to save Keeru's life instead of filing a police report. Father Francis told me that there are two sisters in Lahore, Asma and Hina, both lawyers, who fight the cases of poor people for free. They were the ones who successfully fought the blasphemy case of young Salamat and Barkat Masih in 1995. 'God bless them,' I said. Saeen Manka said, 'If you want your son alive, take him and leave the country.' I begged him to get angry and throw me a bead so my son may be forgiven, but he said, 'Now there is no anger nor grief.' And Baba Khan kept repeating the same words: 'Send him to Karachi today.' 'Why today? He is injured; let him recover, find his strength.' Then Father told me that there were reports of an attack on Keeru and Baba Khan that night.

Now, I give thanks that they managed to get a ticket and medicines for Keeru, and they helped him board the train that very night. Baba Khan also got on a bus to Peshawar. I went and stayed at the church. Father's information was correct; they burned down Baba Khan's house and attacked the clinic that same night. They gave our home to someone else and threw all our belongings on the street.

I woke up and went straight to the bathroom. The damn white man's pot, it was so difficult to sit on it. God bless my son, at least he arranged a lota. It was evening now.

I opened the blue curtains on the big window, and there it was, the blue flower, as large as a cauliflower and with thousands of delicate blue petals. I was standing there, admiring God's creations, when I saw Keeru walk across the yard. There was a girl with him. She was laughing, wearing a fashionable orange salwar kameez, cute designs on the dupatta, a black jersey. I instantly liked her.

'Bebe, this is Aunty Naila,' Keeru said as he entered.

'Assalam-o-alaikum, Mummy-Ji.' She stepped forward, bent down and touched my knees, then she stood up and hugged me. I felt at home, like she was a close relative.

'Aunty did all the arrangements for your arrival—' Keeru started speaking, but I interrupted him. 'Why do you keep calling her Aunty? She's not much older than you!'

They both laughed. Keeru said, 'She's Uncle Raheem's wife, that's why.' 'Oh, okay, she is Raheem's wife. Looks like a young girl, barely a sparrow.' She handed me a bouquet of flowers and said, 'Mummy-Ji, I came to say salaam,' then turned to Keeru and said, 'Sir, you should leave. I will sit with Mummy-Ji for a few minutes, and then I will take the bus back.' Keeru said, 'Aunty, just tell me when you want to leave. I will drop you.'

They go everywhere together, laugh with each other; he calls her Aunty, and she calls him Sir.

He is my son, but you can't really trust any man. Baba Khan used to call me sister, sister, but whenever he got the chance, he would grab my hand, try to hug me. Oh my god, what was I supposed to do? He was the only one trying to protect this poor woman's son. He would bring me a chicken every week. 'Sister,' he would say, 'make a curry out of it. I will get some fresh rotis.' I would make the curry with very little gravy, and he would come and put all the good pieces on his plate, leaving the gizzards, bones and feathers for us. But God bless him, sometimes he would give Keeru a drumstick; Keeru used to love it. I went to Saeen Manka and his companion, Jhoora, too, and asked them for advice. He said, 'Sister, be careful, Baba Khan also has a Jhoora,' and then they both started laughing. I replied, 'He clucks here and lays eggs there.' Finally, one day, when he came after me, I told him, 'Khan, you are my brother. If you behave like a brother, I will serve you, cook for you, but I can't keep doing this because you're giving me a bad name in the neighbourhood.' He said, 'I will marry you.' For a moment, I was left speechless. Keeru's father, Muhammad Hussain, used to hit me so hard when he was angry that I would crash against the wall, my head split open; at times, my neck would get injured, other times, my waist, my shoulders, my hips. He is my son's father, I will always pray for him, but if he hadn't died, I would have. Baba Khan even had a gun. What if he got angry? What would happen to me? I told him, 'No, this solution doesn't work for me.' He got up and left. After that, he would bring the chicken and hand it to me without entering the house. He would come back and pick up the curry. After another year, when Keeru was in school, he changed his path completely. He never came back to our house. But he kept protecting Keeru. He saved his life many times, God bless him.

I am grateful for the day Keeru left the country. It only got worse afterwards. Asia Bibi, Shahzad Bhatti, Governor Taseer, young Ramsha, Mishal Khan, Shama Bibi and Sajjad Masih. I started crying. I prayed that it was in my fate to see the end of this cruelty.

After dropping Naila, Keeru came back and asked if I was feeling tired. I told him, yes, I was still feeling tired, I had just woken up and now I wanted to go back to sleep. Keeru started laughing. My son looks beautiful when he laughs. I hope he spends his life laughing. He warmed some milk for me. I told him to come sit next to me. Then I said, 'I want you to get married soon. Do you like any girl?' He said, 'Bebe, you need to relax, you just got here yesterday.' I said, 'I'm not marrying you off today, am I? I'm just wondering if there is a girl that you like.' He said, 'There's no one.' I said, 'Don't worry, we will find someone.' Then he changed the topic and said, 'Tomorrow is Friday. We are having a party in the evening to welcome you. There will be three or four people, Aunty Naila, Uncle Raheem and my friend, Daljeet.' I told him to invite Baila as well.

'Who's Baila?' he asked. I said, 'The girl who came over.' 'Oh,' he said. 'Isabella; her name is Bella, Bebe, not Baila.' *Whatever,* I thought. *Who cares about such little nuances?* I told him to go to sleep as well; he must be tired from working all day.

He only left after watching me get into bed. He left some water on my bedside table, turned off the big, bright light and turned on a small night light.

My eyes started to water; I wiped them with my hands. My fingers slipped inside the hole, and I remembered the eye; both eyes tear up, but only one can see. I noticed the girls, Naila and Baila, watching my eye, but they didn't say or ask anything. Sometimes, people ask me about it; I tell them that it's been like this from birth. But there's a story behind it. Where should I start and how much should I tell? I never met my parents; they were both murdered during Shia–Sunni riots. People told me that my grandmother hid inside the trunk of a tree with me in her lap, and that's how I was saved. But what's life for a poor orphan? You go here, go there; it's all the same. And on top of it all, my aunt, who raised me, was terrible.

I was just a toddler when my uncle married her. One day, I was sitting in front of the stove with my grandmother, handing her green chillies to grind in the pestle, and my aunt was preparing rotis. My uncle came inside and handed my grandmother ninety-one rupees. He had just been hired as a peon in the post office, and this was his first month's pay. My grandmother put the money away while blessing my uncle: 'May God make eleven out of your one.' My aunt screamed and fell off her stool, leaving the roti burning on the stove. From the very next day, she started chanting 'ninety-one by eleven' 'ninety-one by eleven' at random times and picking fights with my grandmother.

Fourteen years later, when I was eleven years old, she gave birth to her eleventh son. That year, I remember, I was picking guavas from the tree in our yard when something went into my left eye. I yelled and cried. Finally, my aunt came to see what was happening, cursing me the whole time, and then went to consult the local healer. The healer was away finding some medicinal powders in the city, but his wife's aunt said that the most successful remedy for the eye is honey from a small honeybee. On her way back, my aunt checked Khushia's shop, but there was no honey there. Khushia told her that the village nursery had three or four beehives. 'If you need a honeybee, that's where you can find one.' When she got home, my aunt told me to calm down, then she handed each of her four elder sons a piece of dishrag, told them to wrap the cloth around their head and sent them to get a honeybee from the nursery. Fifteen or twenty minutes later, there was commotion in the village. People were running everywhere, and bees were following them. Everyone forgot about me in the commotion. I went inside, crying, and I must have fallen asleep or passed out from the pain. When I woke up, I saw my aunt holding my left eye open with one hand while holding a tong with a live honeybee in the other. Her sons were gripping my hands and feet, so I could not move or get away. I tried my best to break free, but I could not match their strength. She dropped the bee on top of my eye, quickly closed my eyelid and wrapped a cloth around it. I do not remember anything after that. Many days passed, and when I got up from the bed, my left eye was closed. It never opened again.

My aunt insulted and blamed me day and night. She would say that I was already ugly, now I was half blind – 'full of lice, full of bad luck'. She would say that no one would marry me, not even for free. She would refuse to feed me, beat me, and once, she threw a brass glass straight at my face. One afternoon, she handed me her torn, old dress and said, 'Wash your face, wear this dress; you are getting married after evening prayers.' *To whom?* 'Baba Phajja,' she replied. White hair, unable to walk without a stick, and he already had two wives. I made an excuse to go outside and then never looked back. I left, I didn't even take a stalk of husk from them, just the clothes on my body.

If I had not left that day, I wouldn't have ended up at the church, met Muhammad Hussain, given birth to Keeru or arrived here today. I pray and thank God every day for blessing my son. He has given me a new life. People say, cats have nine lives. I say, the poor must have nine lives too. I was given my first life when I was born, the second when I escaped the Sunni–Shia riots, where my parents and half my village were killed, the third when I escaped my aunt's home and landed at the church, the fourth when there was an attack on the church and people burned it down – Keeru was about to be born at the time – and the fifth when Keeru was accused of blasphemy and I sent him to Karachi. I have four left. God will bless me.

Keeru wanted to have the party on Friday in his apartment. He said, 'Bebe, let's do it at my place. I don't want to discomfort you. This way, you can go back and rest in your bed whenever you get tired.' He also wanted to order food from a restaurant. I told him, many times, that we could make the food at home – it's only going to be five or six people. But he insisted that I was still jet-lagged. 'We will make it ourselves for the next party. And,' he said, 'it will not come out of your budget; it's my party.' 'What a fool,' I said. 'Your budget or my budget, it's all your money.'

He also told Naila not to bring anything, but when she arrived, she was holding a cake in her hand, and her husband, Raheem, was holding a bottle of alcohol that he handed to Keeru while trying to hide it from me. Then her husband came towards me, greeted me in a proper Urdu manner, calling me Apa Bi. He seemed like a decent person, spoke Urdu elegantly, looked very attractive, but his white hair made him look much older than Naila. He sat by me. 'Apa Bi,' he said, 'don't worry about anything; I am your brother.' Keeru gave him a glass of alcohol with some juice mixed in it. I felt like teasing Raheem, so I asked, 'What is it?' 'Orange juice,' he replied. I laughed out loud. Even Keeru tried to support his lie, telling me, 'Yes, yes, Bebe, it's orange juice.'

Then came Diljeet, and his energy lit up the room like he hadn't come alone but brought a whole group of people with him. He wasn't wearing a turban, and he was clean-shaven. He looked tall and handsome, about the same age as Keeru. He approached me first. 'Beji, Sat Sri Akaal.' I prayed for him: 'May God bless you.' He put a box of sweets in front of me. 'Beji, congratulations.'

Then someone banged open the door. It was Bella, holding two yellow rolls in her hands. If she looked like a turquoise flower yesterday, she looked like a black panther today. She was wearing a long, black dress that came all the way down to her feet, high heels, her hair was tied in two ponytails on either side of her head, blood-red lipstick, jet-black dot on her forehead and golden glitter on her eyelids. Standing in front of the dining table, she started unrolling the yellow rolls. They turned out to be paper charts with English writing: 'Welcome' on top and 'Canada' on the bottom. On the sides of the charts were drawn two women, one wrapped in a shawl like me and the other wearing a short dress, bare legs, dancing. I said, 'It must be me on one side and Baila on the other side.' But she said, 'No, this is you today, and this is you tomorrow. Look at your hairstyle.' She smiled. I looked where she was pointing – bright pink and green strands of hair flying behind the dancing woman. I looked again at the short dress, barely covering the thighs, naked arms, armpits visible. I burst out laughing. Everyone else was laughing too. Then she said, 'What's in your hand?' and when I looked, the woman in the illustration was holding a wine glass. I laughed so much that my stomach began to hurt. I said, 'Then why tomorrow? Why not today?'

Everyone abruptly stopped laughing. Baila also stared at me.

Keeru and Diljeet looked at each other; their eyes were shining. Then Keeru came close to me and asked, 'Bebe, what should I get you, whiskey, beer or wine?' I said, wine. He asked, 'Red or white?' I said, 'Red.' Keeru brought me a glass, then told Raheem, 'My mother is Christian.'

Naila heard what he said, raised her wine glass and said, 'So am I, a Muslim, drinking sherbet?'

I took a sip; everyone clapped and laughed, raising their glasses high to toast me. Baila put on some English music on her phone and started dancing. Diljeet and Keeru started dancing, too, matching each other's bhangra moves. My son's party started.

I don't know what these kids think. Maybe they think

I am some prim, posh madam who doesn't even know about alcohol. People like me, working people, poor people, we work hard every day to put something in our mouth. I drank bhaang with Saeen Manka and Jhoora, smoked hash, ate opium. You get an alcohol license in Pakistan if you are Christian. I sold the license to the school headmaster so I could get some money, and every year, we had a Christmas party at the church. I tasted red wine for the first time at one of those parties and loved it.

I got hungry after two sips. Chicken korma with pulao, saag greens with corn roti, biryani. My son left no stone unturned for the party. After filling myself with all the food, I started eating the cake. Diljeet looked at Keeru. 'Please,' he said, 'read that poem of yours.' Everyone was surprised.

Raheem said, 'All these years, you never told us you were a poet!'

Keeru's face turned red, but I could tell he was happy. We all asked him to read the poem. He started:

'Kaal'

I nurture an unmet love
for years and decades

together we dance in my heart
breath thumps with your thoughts
for years and decades

these enchanting games of self
meeting the beloved is a nuance of loneliness
for years and decades

lose heart over yourself, girl
and live happily ever after
for years and decades

We all loved it and kept repeating phrases and lines to each other until we started to memorize the whole poem. Then Keeru said, 'If you liked "Kaal", I have also written another poem, "Haal".' Then he read it:

'Haal: Ecstasy'

On the edges of
evening clouds
the glimmer of a setting sun
dances in ecstasy over
the flowing glass surface
of the stream
life does not happen again
and again
dance in ecstasy, friend
an ecstatic dance
the reverberation
of your anklets

dance in ecstasy, friend
an ecstatic dance

Diljeet accompanied Keeru on the guitar. Baila started dancing. Then we all started dancing.

Finally, I fell onto the sofa. I couldn't remember the last time I had danced.

Everyone danced and talked to their heart's content. When I felt exhausted, I made my way back to my apartment. The two girls followed me.

When I got back and sat down, Naila asked, 'Would you like a massage?' Before I could answer, she started pressing my legs. Baila also settled near me. Less than two minutes later, Naila said, 'Mummy-Ji, if you don't mind, will you tell us why you named your son Keeru?'

The good thing about alcohol is that it loosens your tongue, and that is the bad thing about alcohol too.

'Dear daughters, we think insects are inferior, insignificant, but insects know how to survive. They stick to their purpose; they are tough. Small, big, swimming, crawling, flying, there are more kinds of insects than we can count.'

Baila typed something on her phone. Then she read it out loud: 'There are 5.5 million kinds of insects on the planet.'

'Okay,' I said. 'But I can't even imagine a hundred, let alone millions.'

'So you named him Keeru, insect, because there are millions of different kinds of insects?'

'Yes, in a way. I also saw that insects are everywhere, inside and outside. There are germs living inside our bodies. And outside, wherever I have gone, walking, rising, sitting, falling, sleeping, eating, everywhere, at all times, insects have been around me. Even the Bible says it, the Earth belongs to the meek, which means, to the insects, the lowest.'

Baila read from the phone again: 'Blessed are the meek, for they shall inherit the earth. Sermon on the Mount, Matthew 5:5.'

'Yes, that one,' I said. 'When Keeru was in my womb, they killed his father, Muhammad Hussain, because they thought he was Christian. And they set fire to our house while I was still inside. I got out somehow, miraculously. They burned down our whole neighbourhood so they could grab the land. I can't even tell you how many people they killed in just an hour or two. It felt like the last day, like the apocalypse. I was still recovering from this terror when Keeru was born. I used to pray to my darling God, where should I take my son, should I find a hole where I can hide him, where I can protect him from these cruel people. A poor woman's son, no father, he will need to be tough. He was four days old, lying in my lap. I was crying when the words escaped my mouth, "My Keeru," so then, I named him Keeru, son of Muhammad Hussain. Then later, the imam got restless, and we changed it to Keeru Khan, so that's what got stuck.'

The girls were staring at me like they wanted me to say more. What else could I say? Who listens to anyone in this world? And who cares what a poor woman has to say? In that moment, I felt a surge of love for them. I took their hands and went and sat down on the sofa with them.

'Baila, you've done such great make-up; you are a real artist.'

'Yes, Mummy-Ji, it's the work of a make-up artist,' Naila agreed with me.

'Thank you,' Baila said. 'I'll do it for you too.'

'Great,' I said, and she quickly responded, 'Should I do it now?'

'No, not right now,' I told her. 'Do it when Keeru decides to get married.'

'You mean, at his engagement!' Baila jumped up.

When is it? Who is it? The girls were excited. I told them to calm down. 'You must figure out when it is and who it is,' I told them. Their excitement woke me up. *What kind of girl do you want, where will we find her, how will we find her?* We talked and talked. The girls made tea and we ate Diljeet's sweets with the tea.

Then Keeru entered. He said, 'It's late now; everyone should just stay here for the night. Aunty, Uncle has gone to sleep; you can join him.' Then he opened a cupboard and pulled out a thick blanket and a pillow for Baila. My son has everything in the house.

Baila slept on my sofa. Keeru slept on his sofa. He gave one room to Diljeet and the other one to Naila and Raheem. I prayed before sleeping. First, I said Alhamdulillah, then I said Hail Marys on the rosary, and finally, I said Waheguru.

My mother was Sikh. At the time of Partition in 1947, she took a train to go to India, but the train was attacked by Muslims near Gujranwala. They tortured the women, raped them and left them to die. A young man from a nearby village noticed that a woman was alive and brought her home with him. He was the imam of the village's Shia mosque. He treated her injuries, gave her food, and she slowly regained her health, then he converted her to Islam and married her. They had three kids – two sons and me. In 1961, Shia–Sunni riots broke out, and our house was attacked. My parents and both my brothers were killed. I was saved by my grandmother, and she took me to my uncle's house. I ran away from his house when I was fourteen and ended up at the church. There, I converted to Christianity, and they gave me the name Alice. First, they just used to call me Bibi. Then I met Muhammad Hussain. He told me that if I wanted to marry him, the imam would change my name, and he changed my name to Haleema. When my identity card was made, Muhammad Hussain gave my name as Haleema Alice Bibi.

The whole house was asleep when I woke up in the morning. I wanted to see my new neighbourhood. I tiptoed towards the wooden door, opened it and stepped outside. A big, wide street, the same kind of houses on each side, a small tree in each garden. I looked both ways, no cars. I saw the church towards my left and started making my way towards it. The church was in the middle of a field, stairs, a grand, beautiful gate… it all looked impressive. At the intersection, I looked for the mosque and saw it at the corner of the road. It was also big and beautiful; Quranic verses were etched on the walls. I paid my respects to both and turned back. Unknown place, I was afraid of losing my way.

When I entered the house, I could hear people talking. Everyone was awake. They were in my lounge. Keeru and Diljeet were laughing at some joke, Naila was working all alone in the kitchen, and Baila and Raheem were sitting in front of the television.

My darling God, may my son's house always be full of happiness and laughter.

3

NAILA

It's been a couple of weeks since Eid passed. It's Friday today, and it's a holiday on Monday for Canada Day. We are celebrating both holidays together. We had an office party yesterday, and there is a family party today. The family party is at our house, but I'm not too stressed about it. Raheem will do the barbecue, Keeru will bring the pulao and raita, Daljeet will bring saag greens and corn roti, and Bella… who knows about Bella!

I opened the previous job posting for Haleema Enterprises on my phone and started updating it.

I collected all my papers and put them in a box today. I am emptying my desk so Daljeet can start using it. I didn't use the desk very much anyway – just stored all my papers there – but I still felt a little sad when I was vacating it; it was my desk, after all. Actually, I am the one who proposed the idea. It's important for our business to have someone on the sales side. Daljeet already has his own contacts, he has experience with sales, he is well-educated, he has done a course in Microsoft Office, and most importantly, he is a very decent man. He has really made a place for himself here. He introduced himself to all the workers as soon as he got here, and I know he respects me very much. I told him to take my desk. Initially, he refused. 'No, Aunty,' he said, 'I will just bring another chair, and we can share the desk.' Keeru offered to buy a new desk. But I told them that I wanted to stay close to the workroom. The counter is enough for me for now.

Actually, it's not enough, but I have another idea. There's a small storage room next to the workroom – it doesn't have a window, otherwise, it's pretty clean, and it has the same carpet as the rest of the rooms. I am going to turn it into my office. I can go sit there during my lunch break or whenever I need to take time for myself because even though Keeru is very nice and understanding, he is still my boss. I can't rest when he is around. The counter is still better than working in Keeru's office. Anyway, we are really benefiting from Daljeet's arrival. For one, they both arrive together at eight-thirty in the morning now, when it is time to open the warehouse, so I don't have to take the bus at seven in the morning any more. Second, they are both out of the office for at least half of the working day. I can relax properly when they're gone. I finalized the job posting, but I haven't posted it yet. Bella called me in the middle, so I had to talk to her. She wanted to know where she could get some dahi bhalle for the party. Bella is impatient; she requires a lot of attention. Let's see what she wears to the party today.

Our social life has really picked up since Mummy-Ji's arrival. There's a party every weekend, or we take Mummy-Ji out to show her the city – the park, mall, beach. Keeru wants to go camping for two nights next Friday. I've never been camping before; I've only taken day trips to nearby places like Sharon Falls.

I have to update our job postings regularly. Seven out of our ten workers are new refugees or immigrants. Right now, we have women from Syria, Somalia, Iraq, Pakistan and India working with us. This is their first job in Canada. We don't require any skills or experience because I train them all myself. They work for very low wages, and the wages don't go up either. That's why we have new job openings every three or four months. We put up job postings on Craigslist, do the interviews at the office, and that's how we get new workers. We just hired a worker last month, and someone else gave their notice today. It's free to post jobs on Craigslist, otherwise, we would have to put all the money we save on wages towards advertising jobs. This is the only way this business runs profitably.

I uploaded the job posting and walked away from the counter.

It's been three years since I started working here. When I first joined, this business was owned by some white people. The administration was a total mess. It was a small business, but they had five managers: workroom manager, sales manager, marketing manager, office manager, and of course, a general manager. If it was just a matter of giving them a title, it could have worked out, but they all took high salaries. On top of it all, the staff was rude and unpleasant. They would complain all the time, find errors in everything, deduct your pay over the smallest excuses, even start cursing you, calling you 'ignorant' and 'stupid' if you made any little mistake. Of course, the business went bankrupt. They put it up for sale. I had understood the work in my four months there. I knew it could work if it was run properly. But I didn't have the money to buy the business. Raheem was recovering from his accident, he was on disability benefits, we had already taken a loan on the townhouse, and I had this small job that paid very little. No bank would've given us a loan. I didn't know what to do. Keeru came over during the weekend as usual, holding some beer cans and a pizza. I showed him the advertisement for the sale of the business on my phone. He told me that he had no experience running a business. I explained everything to him. I told him that the business worked, the basic plan was sound, there were twelve workers, regular contracts. All that was needed was to reduce the pay for the managers and the business would break even. Raheem also said that it could work. Finally, he supported one of my ideas. Keeru trusts Raheem blindly. He bought the business within a week and hired me as Assistant Manager.

It was a huge challenge for me.

Raheem didn't let me do anything for many years; he really broke my confidence. He wouldn't even let me go to the grocery store alone. He didn't allow me to do a single job, training, course, nothing. When he left for work in the mornings, he used to pack the television cable in his briefcase because he didn't want me to watch anything that I had chosen for myself. There are free newspapers, like *Metro*, at grocery stores, gas stations. If I ever picked one up and started browsing, he would say, 'It's in English. Can you read it?' When I was in Lahore, living with my parents, I had thought, *Yes, he is much older than me, but he has lived abroad for so many years, he must be open-minded.* Actually, I never had much of a choice in the matter. I wanted to finish my education and help my parents run the house, educate my two younger sisters, get them married, see my parents rest and retire. But as soon as I turned sixteen, they started looking for marriage proposals for me. There was a guy in my neighbourhood that I really liked. One day, he asked me to meet him outside, and I went. My father saw me with him. After that, he locked me up in the house. No more school, no more leaving the house, no more friends coming over. I tried to plead with my mother, but my father told me clearly, 'Have mercy on us, just keep quiet, and get married whenever we find a match, and make sure it works. Don't ruin it and come back here. We need to marry the next two daughters as well.' I didn't say anything after that. It's not easy to find marriage proposals for daughters of working-class families like mine. I took two more years to pass my tenth grade, preparing at home and sitting for the exams privately. I got admitted to college, but they found a match for me by then. Raheem is my mother's distant cousin. He was settled in Canada. He came to visit, and that was it. We were married within a month. It took me a year to get my papers, and then I came here. I was only eighteen years old.

My mother is from Karachi, from a family that migrated after Partition; my father is Punjabi. He was a clerk in the Railways Accounts Department when he was posted to Karachi. He was working under my maternal grandfather, whom I have never met. My maternal grandfather owned his own house; he was well-off. They rented a room to my father. That's how he met my mother. They fell in love. When my grandfather found out, he kicked my father out of the house, but he didn't know that as he was kicking my father out of the front door, my mother was leaving the house from the back door. They both met in the street, took a rickshaw, went to the station and caught a train to Lahore, where they settled with my father's family. My mother says that it caused a big fight. They got married, but my mother was never fully accepted by my father's family. She couldn't go back, but she wasn't welcome in her new house either. Both families considered her a slut, a whore, a loose woman, because she had run away from her home. She never met her parents again. She did keep in touch with her sisters.

The truth is that when I first got to Canada, I thought it was a magical place. Raheem was a supervisor in a private security company, we had a two-bedroom townhouse, a car, and all his attention was focused on me. For a while, I was very happy. I got pregnant. But he never let me handle any money, even on Eid; he didn't give me any money, only gifts, and of course, only gifts that he liked. I wanted to get a job, but he said, 'Who's going to give you a job? You can't even run a little house like ours properly.' He was extremely mean, but I didn't mind, or maybe I didn't want to mind. It was only my first year here, and to me, my future – what is it that they say? – looked bright.

Our baby was born. He died two days later. There was a growth in his throat. He couldn't breathe or ingest anything. We both became depressed. Raheem blamed me for the baby's condition, and I blamed him. After that, I couldn't get pregnant again; Raheem blamed me for that too. Then Raheem got into an accident on his way back home from work. His leg was broken in three separate places, and he had injuries on his shoulders and back. We wouldn't have faced as much hardship as we did if the accident had occurred at his workplace.

We only had one support after the accident, Mo, that is, Muhammad Hussain Keeru. What a man! If you look at him, he doesn't look very impressive – dark skin, small eyes, stubby nose; his height and money are the only things that save him. But he is remarkable on the inside – hard-working, intelligent, generous, modest. He used to work three jobs at once when he first got here in 2006. Telemarketing in the morning, security shift in the afternoon and driving a taxi at night. He had this routine for many years. Then he did a real estate course, and eventually, in 2015, he bought his own house. The next year, he bought this business. Very generous…

I often think, *He came to Canada three years after me – I came in 2003, he came in 2006. And look where he is now! I am stuck in the same place where I started. A tenth-grade education, nothing in my name.*

No one holds Keeru in higher regard than me. He never misbehaves with the workers. Even if someone makes a mistake, he doesn't lose his temper. Last year, when Dasveer had her second baby, he told her to take three months off. When Raheem needed surgery for his leg, I was away from work for two or three days. Dasveer supervised the workroom in my absence. She used the wrong material for an order. Of course, there's no bigger mistake in our trade. She called me out of desperation. She said, 'Didi, please, come now, I don't know what to do.' We hadn't sold our car yet. I got in the car and came straight to the office.

When I got there, Dasveer looked pale; she was trembling. Five hundred sheets; it was a loss of thousands of dollars. I went to Keeru's office and showed him the sample. Keeru kept looking at the sample, checked the order on his computer, looked through his files. Then he stood up, told me to come outside with him. And what did he say to Dasveer when we went out? 'Dasveerji! I am going to raise your salary next month.' Dasveer went even paler when she heard this. Keeru continued, 'You are going to help me sell this order, which means you are going to get a lot of sales experience, so your salary is naturally going to go up.' Dasveer laughed, then started crying. He told me to make some fresh coffee. When Dasveer stopped crying, he went out to get some samosas to go with the coffee. Samosas? We were both surprised. Then I remembered that Dasveer was pregnant, and a few days ago, she was craving samosas, kept talking about how she really wanted to eat samosas. Keeru must have heard her.

Later, I asked him about it, and he said, 'Aunty, it's my fault too. I'm too used to you, so I never left my office to check what was happening in the workroom even once. If you were here, the mistake would've been corrected immediately.' He really appreciates my work. And he has a lot of business sense. He set up a meeting with me and Dasveer later that same day. He told us to figure out overtime for all the workers so we could finish the order and meet the client's deadline, then we would sell this item at wholesale price without any limits on the quantity. He handed us all a sheet, and said, 'This is a sample. You will get it for fifteen dollars; you can sell it at whatever rate you like.' We knew that the same item sold at the store for sixty, so we could easily sell it for thirty. Dasveer said that her husband worked at a clothing store in Payal Centre. Keeru gave her two sets for him so he could sell them in the shop. I asked Keeru if we would have to buy the sheets with cash, and after some thinking, he said that each worker could take five sheets on a two-week credit basis. We all took five sheets. I sold all five in my townhouse complex within a week. Now I sell one or two items every week. Working with Keeru, for the first time ever, I opened my own personal bank account and started depositing money in it. I want to become Keeru's business partner, and I know he likes the idea too.

Once I met Mummy-Ji, I realized where Keeru gets his intelligence from. She's also simple and wise like him. She said, 'Why do you call her Aunty? She's not that much older than you!' She wants to find a match for Keeru. And I know she really likes me. If Raheem wasn't in the picture, she would've wanted me to marry him.

Would I have married him?

Keeru is a very decent man. When he bought his house, I thought, *Maybe I'll get my younger sister married to him.* I asked Raheem about it, and he said that Keeru is a gem, a diamond, but he is a musalli, a low-caste. Oh god, no, no way, my family would never agree to marry into a musalli family. I like Keeru a lot, I respect him immensely, but more than that? I can't even imagine. Raheem knows how I feel. That's why he's so relaxed with him. Anyway, he is younger than both of us, also darker than both of us. We are syeds, he is a musalli. Raheem thinks he is better than Keeru.

What's the truth? The truth is that Keeru is a far superior human than Raheem. If Raheem even gives someone two dollars, he will remind them and hassle them so much that they'll feel humiliated until they return it. On the other hand, Keeru paid two months of our mortgage to save the house from foreclosure. We haven't been able to pay him back yet, but Keeru has never asked us – neither me nor Raheem – about it.

By the time I posted the job advertisement and took a round of the workroom, Keeru and Daljeet had left. I opened the storeroom. Our new materials were lying in the front of the room, and most of the back of the room was covered with old, discarded materials. I thought there were two industrial shelves, but there were actually four shelves hidden below the piles of cloth. I went to the storeroom and asked if any worker was done with their quota and if they could come help me for ten minutes. Dasveer said, 'Didi, clear up some space near the door. We will bring out the cloth, vacuum the room and set it up for you.' All the workers paused their work and came to help. They cleared the room in ten minutes. We put a fan there and left the door open.

We sorted all the cloth that was now piled outside. Plain, floral, stripes, edgings, buckram, laces… all of them went in separate boxes. We adjusted the shelves and arranged the boxes of cloth on them in such a way that they could be seen clearly and reached conveniently.

It was late by the time I finished everything, but I was satisfied with the work.

It would cost us ten to fifteen thousand dollars if we went to the market to buy all this stuff today. I don't have a shop where I can sell the same sheets week after week. In my townhouse complex, most people own their homes, so they are not going to leave unless they sell the place, which means I must cater to the same set of customers all the time. But we do have everything here – machinery, materials, operators. If we wanted, we could make a lot of different items. It's true that ten thousand dollars' worth of material can be turned into a value of at least a hundred thousand dollars within a year.

If I can manage such a turnaround on my own, I'm sure I will be Keeru's business partner by next year.

Uff! It's very exciting.

It was seven in the evening by the time I reached home. I was completely exhausted, but I felt great about the day's work. I was ready to enjoy the party. I opened the door and entered. Raheem was sitting on a sofa in the living room.

'You found the time to visit your own home?' Then

he started ranting, 'The guests are almost here, the barbecue hasn't started, it's too much, I don't know what you want. We have invited good people...' and on and on he went.

I placed my bag on the table, opened the balcony door, dragged the barbecue closer to the room, took off its cover, opened the toolbox and put it next to the barbecue. Then I went to the kitchen, opened the fridge and took out the trays of chicken and lamb, which I had left there to marinate last night. This whole time, Raheem kept raging, kept blabbering; he didn't stop for a single minute. The 'good people' we had invited devolved into 'Punjabi assholes', and I became a 'slut'. He sat up there, feeling superior, while he cut me to pieces with the sharp elegance of his language.

I felt like my heart was going to explode in my chest. I ran upstairs, entered the bathroom and locked the door behind me. I turned on the tap in the sink and turned on the exhaust fan. By this time, I was sobbing and crying, the tears running down my face like a thread. Every day, I go through this experience.

Every. Day.

I leave the house at seven-thirty in the morning and return home at six-thirty. Whether I come back on time or not, whether there is a party at home or not, I have to listen to his insults, curses and sarcasm. If I say anything back to him, he completely loses his mind and gets uncontrollably angry. I get even more scared. I think my heart really will explode one day listening to him and enduring his behaviour towards me.

I don't want this life.

The bell rang. I hurriedly washed my hands, swept back the hair that had fallen on my face and splashed some water on it, took out the lipstick from my bag and started putting it on my lips. Then I came out of the bathroom and changed my clothes as quickly as possible. I ran downstairs to open the door.

Raheem had already opened it. Mummy-Ji and Bella were standing on the balcony, watching the evening spread out before them.

'I just got Keeru's text. He and Daljeet will be thirty minutes late,' Raheem told me.

I didn't respond to him, didn't even look his way.

I can't find the strength to listen to the voice inside my heart that keeps telling me that I hate this person. I am as scared of this voice as I am of Raheem. Eventually, the bigger fear will eat the smaller fear. Hopefully, that will be the moment of my deliverance.

Mummy-Ji saw me. As she approached me, she saw inside me too. She hugged me in such a way that I felt like I was protected, safe, like my heart might not explode after all.

'Blessed daughter, may you stay safe from the evil eye, may your fortune soar higher and higher.' She kept me in her embrace.

A few tears appeared in my eyes, and soon, I was crying in her arms.

'Some people are very dramatic. Our Naila can compete with anyone,' Raheem announced, as if to no one, just speaking into the room.

No one responded to him.

Bella came towards us and embraced us both. I felt the warmth of both their bodies envelop me. In this warmth, there was love, confidence, strength.

I wiped my tears and stood up straight.

'Mummy-Ji, what will you drink? Should I get some wine?' I asked.

'No, daughter, my soul doesn't want alcohol today. Can you bring me some juice?'

'Don't worry, Aunty, I'll get it.' Bella had already reached the kitchen. Then she asked me, 'Will you have some juice too?'

'Yes, please.'

'I missed you,' Bella said.

I saw her properly for the first time since I had come downstairs – blue jeans and a thin, flowing rainbow-coloured top. 'I like your top,' I told her.

'Thank you, I got it from the Surrey Central Mall, at the Pride Festival.'

'The one that happened at Surrey Central Mall yesterday?' Raheem suddenly spoke up.

He can't hear or something now – that's what she just said.

Bella nodded.

'There are children, women, families at the mall. What was the point of spreading such obscenity there?'

Bella lost it completely. She raised her voice. 'It was necessary to do it at the mall because some people still think that gay culture is obscene. They don't want to accept it as a part of society.'

Raheem also raised his voice in response, and they started arguing with each other. I could tell Raheem was getting dangerously heated; he was now shaking with anger.

'Are you homophobic too?' Bella looked at me like she was accusing me.

'No, but I… I think it's unnatural,' I said.

'I can't take this bullshit.' She threw the car keys in front of Mummy-Ji and left.

'Bella! Take the car with you.' Mummy-Ji got up to go after her, but she had already left. 'Naila, give her the car keys; throw them from the balcony.'

I picked up the keys and went to the balcony. Bella was exiting the housing complex. I called her, and she looked up. I threw the keys near her. She picked them up.

Bella can't tolerate anything that goes against her temperament for even a minute. You can't spend life this way.

Then how do you spend life? Like me? Just keep tolerating everything, year after year after year. I came here in 2003. I have spent sixteen years tolerating this man's insults. I am now thirty-four years old. What sins am I paying for?

The fire in the barbecue was starting to pick up. I kept standing there and watching it. Smoke, smoke. The coals need to turn red before we throw the meat on it.

Raheem picked up his crutches to come outside on the balcony. I went back inside.

Keeru and Daljeet arrived. They brought pulao, saag and alcohol with them. They were laughing when they entered, but when they saw the atmosphere inside, they fell silent, like us.

Was it a party or torture? If Mummy-Ji wasn't there, I would have gone upstairs.

Daljeet had brought his guitar, but nobody sang.

Everybody ate a little bit out of politeness. I packed some food for Bella, and I gave them the remaining pulao and saag to take back.

When they left, I went upstairs and took two sleeping pills. Then I turned off my cell phone, went to the second bedroom, and fell on the mattress.

My eyes opened. The sun was falling on my face. I got up, but my head was spinning, so I sat down again. I saw the blue, shining sky from the window, I just wanted to sit there and look outside. When my head stopped spinning,

I walked towards the window – the green grass of the park in front of our house, flowers, tall trees.

This room is peaceful.

I wanted to go to the bathroom. I kept planning it in my head for a long time. I finally gathered the courage and opened the door. I could hear the television. Raheem was downstairs. I went and used the bathroom upstairs, returned, drew the curtains and sat back on the mattress. *Today is Saturday,* I told myself, and then I went back to sleep.

It was completely dark when I woke up again. I opened the door just a little bit. I could still hear the television. Raheem was not in his bedroom.

My mind was foggy from the pills; I couldn't make sense of anything. I took two more pills and retreated into the room again.

I woke up early in the morning. Cold sunlight; drops of dew on the grass, sometimes golden, sometimes silver. I felt calmer. I turned on my cell phone and charged it. There were ten or twelve messages. Seven messages from Raheem, sent during the night; I skipped them. Three from Bella and one from Keeru. The three messages from Bella:

Yesterday morning: *Bebe is asking if you are okay.*

Afternoon: *Bebe is asking if you are feeling well.*

Evening: *Bebe is very worried, call now.*

At night, Keeru had sent a message: *Aunty, please call us, we are all very worried.*

We are all very worried.

We. All of us.

I couldn't see through the tears in my eyes. I thought of them one by one – Keeru, Mummy-Ji, Bella, Daljeet. Dasveer. My neighbour. The workers at the warehouse.

The tears kept coming to my eyes like I was feeling an unknown happiness, like my heart's blocked veins were finally opening. It was a strange feeling. Both grief and happiness were mixed with each other, becoming one. In my misery, when I didn't even feel the desire to live any longer, the knowledge that I was valued made me feel like I had discovered a treasure.

The treasure inside me, the treasure of my own self. Me.

Even my parents weren't happy at my birth. If I had been a son, my mother could've strengthened her position with her in-laws. My father could've eased his worries. They lost their chance to better their lives because of me, and so they never approached me with love. I always felt like they weren't my real parents. After me, my parents had two more daughters, and they acted the same way with them. My mother blamed herself for running away from her family, and she decided that she would condemn all her daughters to the old ways to protect them from her own fate. Nobody hugged anybody at my house, nobody even smiled at anyone. Children who don't experience their parents' love are left with an absence inside them.

Only they are aware of this absence. They spend all their lives filling that absence, but it never goes away. All their life, no matter who they are with, no matter where they are, they try and hide the absence. It tires them out.

When I got married and came here, I suddenly acquired a house where I could do some things as I pleased. I also acquired nice clothes, jewellery, a lot of make-up, silk panties, lace bras, expensive perfumes, and most of all, sex. The permission to have sex. It kept me occupied for many months. I call sex my 'Third World' – hehehe – it's still 'backwards' but on the 'path of development'. All this was enough to satiate me. I didn't let Raheem's insults affect me too much. I was hurt by them, of course, but it's like I didn't allow myself to acknowledge that I was hurt. Once, I must have been six months pregnant, there was a party at the house of his white boss. He called me from the office and told me to get dressed because he didn't want to be late. But when he came home, he said that he'd go alone. When I asked why, he said, 'You don't have any manners, you don't even know how to talk. You speak Punjabi when you try to speak Urdu, you can't speak a single correct English sentence, you dress like an illiterate, uncivilized person. How can I take you anywhere?'

The issue of language – how does Bella put it? – confuses me. My aunts tell me that I don't speak proper Punjabi, my in-laws think that I don't speak proper Urdu, Raheem and all the white people here think that I can't speak proper

English. What's the message I get from everyone? It's that I know three languages, but I can't speak any of them.

But I speak all three. I can speak all three. I *do* speak all three.

The people who have a problem with how I speak, I think, just don't want to listen to what I have to say.

I get this complaint only when I challenge them, when I say something they don't want to hear, when I say something that doesn't please them. Whether it is Raheem, the cashier, my aunts… they never find errors when I'm saying things they like; they only correct me when they stop agreeing with what I'm saying. If Raheem is in a good mood, or he wants something from me, he doesn't have any problem with how I speak Urdu. The other day, I was at Sears, getting bedsheets for Mummy-Ji. I tried to make a little conversation with the cashier. I said, 'Very nice weather.' She said, 'Wish I was at the beach.' I agreed: 'Same here.' She was wearing a nose ring, so I complimented her, 'Pretty nose ring.' While thanking me, she scanned a sheet twice, but when I pointed it out to her, she said, 'No, I didn't.' I told her to check again. Her supervisor came. The supervisor checked, and it turned out that she had made a mistake and I was right, but she said to the supervisor, 'Her English is so bad, I couldn't tell what she was saying.'

I was speaking with my aunt on the telephone. We had been talking for half an hour. She was telling me about my uncle, I was speaking about Raheem, then she started complaining about my mother. I said, 'Why are you gossiping about my mother with me?' She paused for a minute and then said, 'Gossip is not a proper Punjabi word.' I said, 'You can use whatever word you like, but first answer my question.' She said, 'You are over thirty now, but you still can't speak Punjabi properly,' and slammed the phone.

I think, they don't like the questions I ask, and they don't want to answer them, so they tell me to shut up, or they start finding problems with my language. We don't want to hear you / you can't speak properly. Your words have no value / you don't know the language.

Actually, I have realized that these people don't want to recognize the truth of my existence. They don't want to accept that every person's language is a history of their existence. Instead of recognizing me, they say, go change your history before we hear what you have to say. Only the kings of the world, the ones with all the power, can dismiss people in this manner. I feel like I am standing in front of some Mughal royalty. Only the powerful can dismiss the organic relationship between someone's language and their existence, their history, their life. Look at my example: I was born and raised in Punjab, my mother tongue is Urdu, I was not allowed to study after tenth grade, and I was married off to an Urdu-speaking man when I was eighteen and sent to Canada. My husband doesn't even allow me to leave the house. So, I use these three languages the best I can. What else can I do? You will hear my voice in three languages.

The sun kept rising. I picked up my phone and texted Bella: *Thank you to Mummy-Ji. Will call soon.*

I opened Raheem's messages at the end: *Please forgive me, I am ashamed, I have no one but you.* Etcetera, etcetera. His respectable and proper language humiliated me more than anyone could ever do with even the vilest curses and insults. I didn't text him back.

There has always been a single bed, a nightstand, a chair and a desk in this room. I dragged the bed all the way to the window. Then I brought my clothes, papers, toothbrush, make-up and everything else that belonged to me over here from the master bedroom. I hung my clothes in the closet, arranged my papers on the desk, put everything in its place.

I was feeling hungry, but I didn't want to face Raheem, so I kept arranging the room.

I found a poster among my things, a poster I had brought with me from Lahore. It showed a woman dancing in the fields. Raheem didn't approve of it, so I never put it up. I taped the poster on the wall between the door and the closet. A few years back, my younger sisters sent me a beautiful embroidered shawl. I hung it up on the wall opposite the door.

I couldn't ignore my hunger any longer. I almost called Bella to ask her to bring me some food. I knew she would bring it too. But there was food in the house; she would have to bring it all the way from her place. I had to face Raheem at some point. I would have to do it on my own.

I lay back down on the bed – still hungry.

I didn't have the strength, or desire, to confront Raheem.

My phone's screen lit up. It was a text from Raheem. *I warmed some food. Come and eat it.*

Eat with Raheem? Forget it!

I texted back: *Thank you. Not hungry.*

Usually, Raheem goes to bed by eleven. When I went down after eleven, the television was still blaring, and Raheem was sleeping on the sofa bed with all the lights on.

I took lamb chops, chicken drumsticks, two naans, some red chutney and a box of orange juice from the fridge and went upstairs.

Raheem never goes to bed without turning off the lights. *I'll turn them off before going upstairs,* I thought, but then I just left them as they were.

The next day was Monday, 1st July, Canada Day.

In 1867, on this day, three English provinces joined to make Canada.

On this day, this very land on which I now live was stolen from Indigenous people. The victory of imperialism and the defeat of indigeneity. The victory of the powerful and the defeat of the oppressed.

But in my home, on 1 July 2019, the powerful were defeated and the oppressed won.

After today, I told myself, *Raheem will never insult me.*

If he does, I will leave.

There are shelters here, and now Mummy-Ji is here too.

4

DALJEET

These days, day and night, we work extra hard. In the morning, I come to the warehouse with Keeru, I sit at Aunty Naila's table and chair, open my laptop, start working. First, I scour each local British Columbia newspaper to find ads asking for every type of linen, sheets, curtains, blankets, drapes, anything related to our work, and when I find one or two, I put together a quote and send it. It's the same today. I am putting together quotes, and Keeru is working at his desk.

It's been two weeks since the Eid party at Aunty's house, three months since Be-Ji's welcome party – I am still here. I spoke with my bee-ji in Chandigarh over the phone, spoke with my brother-in-law in Chilliwack too… Everything is fine on both sides… as fine as it can be.

After the Eid party at Aunty's house, our parties have stopped, the camping programme has been cancelled. Keeru and I were late to arrive at the party that day. When we arrived and entered Aunty's living room, a tense and heavy fog was settled in the room. Uncle was sitting in front of the TV, brooding, just the way my father would sit in front of the TV after coming home from work – he didn't get up to welcome us, he didn't even look at us. Aunty looked like she had been crying. Be-Ji had fallen asleep on the sofa. Bella was nowhere to be seen. Keeru and I looked at each other; something had happened.

We sat with Uncle and gulped a can of beer each, ate some barbecued chicken and hurriedly made our escape. We were quiet on the way back home – so was Be-Ji. Keeru asked what had happened. She responded that Bella got mad at Raheem and left. Keeru asked why she got mad. Be-Ji said it was something about a 'top'; they were speaking too quickly, so she didn't understand much. We arrived home, and Be-Ji's car was parked outside. Bella was inside the house, shrouded in a blanket, her face hidden. Be-Ji went to her room; we made our way to Keeru's apartment.

It felt like all our truths were out in the open now. We were all together before, partying all the time. Whatever work we did, inside the house or outside, we laughed our way through it. We spent the evenings with each other, sharing food and drinks, singing and dancing, chatting and getting to know each other. It all felt like a big, festive carnival. But the carnival ended at Aunty Naila's house. We didn't end it. Who knows who ended it, why it ended.

Everyone's depression bolted out of its confines and came knocking at their doors that night. My own monstrous depression attacked me, mouth agape, merciless.

We – Keeru and I – were afraid to be alone with our thoughts. We didn't go to our rooms. We took the two sofas in the living room and slept on them. TV on, lights on, phone on, laptop on. The whole night, I was awake with my eyes shut.

Then everyone got busy. Be-Ji started English language classes. She would come back at three, exhausted, and go to bed around seven or eight when Keeru and I returned from work. Aunty became solemn. Bella slept day and night, at random hours. Then she got up, suddenly full of energy. For two days, she looked for jobs, applied for jobs, interviewed for jobs, even got the jobs, but she couldn't keep the jobs. She fought with her managers, or she complained that her co-workers treated her differently. She got depressed again, unable to get off the sofa.

We are four siblings. Didi is the eldest, then me, then Manpreet and Sukhveer. Here, people tell me I am good-looking, but I think to myself that if these people ever saw my Bee-Ji they would really know the meaning of good-looking. All four of us pale in comparison to her – she still radiates an attention-grabbing beauty.

Bapu-Ji and Bee-Ji live on their lands, which have now come close to the territory of Chandigarh, or the territory of Chandigarh has come close to them. Bapu-Ji takes pride in his high status as a landowner. He wants me to emulate him, take pride in our status. He was very strict with me – walk like this, talk like this, behave like this. I wanted to cut my hair. I asked Bapu-Ji; he was furious, started shouting at me. He told me clearly, 'If you cut your hair, don't come back to this house.' Then Bee-Ji came to my defence. She told him, 'Why are you fighting with the boy? He's been scratching his head; probably got something from the kids at school. Let him get well. Hair will grow back in three months.' Bapu-Ji backed off. But he never liked me after that.

I cut my hair, took off my turban, but I didn't show my face to Bapu-Ji for two months out of fear.

We all knew I couldn't stay there for long.

How did I come to Canada? Bee-Ji requested my brother-in-law, pleaded and begged. He wouldn't agree; he would say, 'It's very tough to settle in Canada.' Two days before their return to Canada, when Didi, Bee-Ji, and Bapu-Ji were sleeping, my brother-in-law brought a bottle of whisky and sat down with me. He kept telling me, 'Canada's economy isn't the same, jobs are scarce, they don't want to hire us for the few available jobs. Anyway, there's rising inflation.' Then he said, 'Man to man, let me tell you something. Don't tell anyone else, promise me.' I promised. He continued, 'If I bring you on a work visa, the cost is forty thousand dollars, twenty thousand on the points system. You will have to pay it back in two to three years. This is the rate everywhere in BC and Vancouver.' 'How do people pay back such a big amount?' I asked him. 'They can do it; that's why it's the rate,' he told me. I said, 'If everyone can do it, I will do it too.'

My brother-in-law taught me how to put together a quote. Maybe it doesn't cost twenty thousand dollars to learn this, but truthfully, it's a very useful skill. The market rate, the production expenditure, the cost of buying, the cost of selling, the profit margin – you must pay attention to all these things if you are putting together a competitive quote. When I arrived in Canada, I got lucky with one thing: I got a hospital contract from my first few quotes. It was a fat contract. My commission was substantial. I sent some money to Bee-Ji, paid the debt incurred for the flight to Canada, bought this laptop, bought a phone and a guitar. I felt good. It gave me confidence. After the hospital contract, I got one or two other jobs, but the year is going empty otherwise. In April, Bapu-Ji is scheduled for a liver surgery; next September, my younger sister, Manpreet, is getting married. That's at least ten thousand right there. I also have to give my brother-in-law at least five. Obviously, I must budget my own expenses too.

The worry is making me anxious. I find it hard to breathe, and sometimes, I feel like I'm about to have a panic attack.

I really appreciate Bella. At least, she accepts that she feels depression and anxiety. I don't admit it or share it with anyone. I came to Canada to escape my depression. Chilliwack was a small city – few jobs and even fewer chances to grow a business. I was away from my family. And I didn't like living in my brother-in-law's house. I didn't appreciate his mother's behaviour towards me. At first, she was super nice. 'Daljeet, eat this, eat that.' She showed me a lot of love. Then she started giving me jobs and tasks – giving me duties related to her daughter. 'Daljeet, drop Baby there, take her shopping, pick her up from her friend's place.' Honestly, I am a little scared of Baby. She is eccentric like Bella, but she calls me a villager, a country bumpkin, a creep. Bella is eccentric, but she cares for me, she smiles at me, she talks to me.

I asked Keeru, 'Why does Baby call me a creep?' He started laughing. 'You must stare at her,' he told me. I thought about it. I do look at her, but I don't stare.

It got too tense in Chilliwack. I was also worried that my actions would reflect on Didi. Maybe they would blame her for me living there. I was looking for ways to get out. It was my good luck that I found these people. Keeru responded to my brother-in-law's notice with a forthright cover letter. My brother-in-law gave the job to someone else, but I remembered his name, Keeru. It's a strange name. Then, one day, I was visiting my cousin, Amarjeet, in Surrey. We were going to his friend's place. On the way, he said, 'We have some free time; let's check out the Punjabi Writers' Gathering at Newton Library. The Indian poet Surjeet Patar is reading too.' I had heard Patar many times before, but I was curious about the

Punjabi literary scene around here. I immediately noticed that I wasn't the only one in the room without a turban or long hair – there were many others like me. Surjeet Patar presented his poem, *'Mulaqat'* – Meeting. I liked this part the most:

> You and I met
> Rain falling on a burning jungle

I heard the poems of many local poets for the first time – poets like Ajmer Rode, Surjeet Kalsi, Sadhu Binning – all of them excellent, all of them politically engaged. I also appreciated that both the male poets were clean-shaven. I wanted to meet them, but Amarjeet felt it was getting late. We were about to leave when the name of the next poet was announced: Muhammad Hussain Keeru. I told Amarjeet to wait just one minute. I heard the poem. *He is talented,* I thought. He was a young guy, probably around my age. Businessman and poet. I felt like there was something there.

A stream of thoughts kept spinning around my head even after I got back to Chilliwack – I kept seeing him, thinking about him. I read his cover letter again. There is no harm in trying. So I called him. We spoke. He said, 'Everyone calls me Mo.' I laughed. They call every Muslim man 'Mo' here. Many Muslims have Muhammad as their first name, which gets shortened to Mo. White people want to turn me into 'Dil', I prefer 'Jeetu'; that works for them too. 'Nice name, yeah,' they tell me.

I have found peace here in Surrey.

Amarjeet is my cousin, but his house feels strange to me and so does his family. They keep talking to each other in English, keep eating, keep drinking, keep making calls on their phones like I am not even there. They give their votes to PC – it's the party of people like Modi here. I had to share the bedroom with Amarjeet. He plays hard rock, techno or rap all night on the speakers. It's not my taste in music. I like ghazals and slower, melodious songs. Jagjit and Chitra-Ji, Satinder Sartaj, Lata-Ji, Mehdi Hassan-Ji – these are some of my favourites. I try to copy all of them, learn from them, including Mehdi Hassan-Ji. I am spending my time composing Keeru's poem, 'Kaal', these days. Copying is not enough for me any more. I always wanted to compose my own song – now I've found the song. It feels like my heart has found a language, my feelings have found words.

After I am done putting together quotes, I start looking at a list of shops. We have contacted and delivered products to twenty local shops in two weeks. An average of two shops a day. I want to continue this pace for the next three months.

Three months. I have thirty dollars left in my account. I can't ask Didi; she is under my brother-in-law's influence, and she has been a little reserved with me. She doesn't know about our 'man-to-man' arrangement, so she thinks that he has done us a massive favour. He has done us a favour, yes, I agree. But it's not exactly how Didi, Bee-Ji, and Bapu-Ji think it is. I qualified for the point system because Didi is here, my brother-in-law gave me a place to stay, gave me training, gave me a chance to do some business. It's been almost a year, and I've stayed at their place pretty much the whole time. I slept in their living room. I paid my expenses, but still – I was living in their home.

My financial situation is really tough right now. I am debating pawning my guitar. I can't do without the laptop, but I could get a hundred, maybe a hundred and fifty dollars, if I sell the guitar. I should have a little money in the account at least. I googled some pawnshops in the area and started searching for guitar prices.

'Daljeet, do you have a few minutes?' Keeru walked towards me, holding a paper in his hand.

'Yes, of course.' Sometimes he calls me Daljeet, sometimes Jeetu – I like it both ways. And Be-Ji thinks my name is 'Diljeet', which means the one who wins hearts, so every time Be-Ji sees me, she says, 'Here comes the winner of hearts,' but she doesn't know that Bapu-Ji named me 'Daljeet', which means victorious army, the army that conquers and wins battles. I laugh to myself instead of correcting her – no one else has corrected her yet either. I find it endearing. Maybe I should be Diljeet?

'Good news; the orders are starting to come.' Keeru smiled at me and put the paper on my desk. 'It's a small order, but you deserve all the credit. This is all because of your hard work.'

It was an order of ten sets of sheets. 'Very good,' I said. 'Are the items ready?'

'I will ask Aunty to get them ready.' He bent forward to pick up the order sheet and saw the guitars on my laptop screen. 'Are you buying a new guitar?'

'Maybe,' I said. 'First, I will sell the old one.'

'Really?' He continued, 'Please don't sell it. The house will feel so boring.' Then he turned and walked towards the door. 'I will get the order ready.'

I watched him as he walked away.

When I think of selling the guitar, I also feel like life will become boring.

'I heard someone say "order". Is there some good news?' Aunty entered the room before Keeru could leave.

'Yes, Aunty, congratulations. We got an order for ten sets of sheets.' Keeru handed the paper to Aunty. 'You get the order ready, and we will deliver it.'

'Okay, sir, perfect, give me ten minutes.' She walked out of the room.

I felt excited about the order, but my situation was the same. I was still worried about money, still anxious, still on the verge of a panic attack. I closed the laptop and put it in my backpack, took my phone and cleared the desk.

We will not return here after the delivery. Aunty will lock up the warehouse.

Keeru took the box with the order from Aunty, and we started walking towards the door.

'Daljeet, one minute,' Aunty called me.

'Yes?' I turned.

'This is your pay for two weeks… advance, cash.' She handed me an envelope.

I looked. Five hundred dollars.

'The accountant is asking for the scale, then he can make a balance cheque,' she told Keeru.

'Okay, we will send it today or tomorrow.'

Then we left and got into the car.

The weather changed, inside and outside, in a moment.

I started singing Jagjitji's song. *'Dhai din na jwani naal chaldi / kurti mulmul di.'* Keeru provided the groove, tapping the steering wheel.

Our first order on the back seat, five hundred dollars in my pocket, a sweetheart next to me, we matched the song and beat the whole way.

I used to think Keeru was some deep soul for picking the pen name 'Keeru', but then I realized it was his actual name, what Be-Ji called him. Maybe they have this name in West Punjab, but I have never heard it on our side. It's a little awkward saying his name. He doesn't look like a

'Mo' – no beard, no moustache, no mosque cap. I hesitate to say 'Keeru'; it still feels like an insult. This is not just my problem. Other than Be-Ji, everyone feels the same. This is why Aunty always calls him, 'sir' and Bella, 'partner'. One day, I was talking to Bella, and she said that Bebe gave him the name Keeru because there are five million kinds of insects, because insects are survivors, tough, strong, because the Bible says the world belongs to them. When Be-Ji says Keeru, it sounds like a proper name; when anyone else says it, it sounds weird, offensive, like we are calling him an insect, a pest, a worm, vermin or something. But I know one thing for sure – he is a good person. Yesterday, he opened an Excel sheet on his laptop and showed it to me. He said, 'This is my pay scale; this is everyone else's. Now tell me where you want to go on the scale.' I asked him what he thought about it. He said, 'You should charge according to your need right now.' I thought, five hundred rent, five hundred expenses, one thousand savings, that's my need, so I said, 'Two thousand, after taxes.' He simply said, 'Okay.' Then I wanted to confirm the rent with him, but he said, 'Five hundred is a lot for one person. You should wait and start paying rent when the work situation is settled.' I did not agree, so he just said okay. He says okay a lot. I like his language; they speak a sweet-sounding Punjabi. But he says, 'Daljeet, I like your Punjabi more.' He likes the word 'sahmat': agree. He says he will use it in his poems.

This week, we received four orders and added another ten outlets. We were also busy setting up the office, so we couldn't visit a lot of shops. On Sunday, Keeru and I went to an auction to buy an office chair and a desk for me. There, we also looked at some furniture that had arrived from a corporate office – it was made of wood and leather, brown and black. The salesman assured us that it was 'as good as new'. It included two swivelling office chairs, two desks, eight regular chairs, a round conference table and one bookshelf. All for $340. We realized that the leather was fake, but we still bought everything. The next day, Keeru's office looked completely transformed with all the furniture. It now serves as our joint office, as well as the conference room.

Today, at 5 p.m., we will meet for the first time as a group at the office. We will review our performance for the past three months and plan for the next three. Me, Keeru, Aunty and Dasveer.

I didn't know what to expect from the meeting – but what happened surprised me.

Keeru began the meeting. 'I have worked with Aunty Naila for two and a half years, with Dasveer for two years and with Daljeet for three months. I consider this good luck, and I am also very proud of our work. I consider it my good luck because I feel I am working with three of my best friends, and I am sure all of you also know how good it feels to work amongst friends. And I am proud because we make a great team, a winning team. In three months, we have established our own retail sales network, and we are beginning to get a steady flow of orders. If we maintain our current speed, we will soon become profitable.'

'Didi, I told you we'll make a profit this year,' Dasveer said.

'Yes, Dasveer knew this was going to happen. She told me when we got the very first order for ten sheet sets,' Aunty said.

'I completely agree with you, Dasveer; this year, we are going to make a profit. Not just me, all four of us. As a result, I would like to request Daljeet to take the position of sales manager, Dasveer to become the workroom supervisor, and Aunty can take the role of business manager. I will continue as the general manager. Our pay scale will stay the same for now, but we will review it all next year.' He opened his briefcase, brought out four short piles of paper and placed one in front of each of us. He continued, 'I just met with our lawyer, and right now, as it stands, this is one person's company, but now I want it to become our company. I want all of you on the board. The lawyer suggests a breakdown of seventy, ten, ten, ten. If this does not sound good to you, we can discuss it with him. He's going to have a meeting with all four of us soon.'

'Sir, you always amaze me.' Aunty stood up and started eating the samosas we were saving for later. 'It's incredible how big your heart is!'

'Aunty, this has nothing to do with my heart; this is common sense. This business will not survive in the long run if we don't take this step.' He picked up a samosa as well. 'I would have never taken over this business or any other business if it wasn't for Aunty and Uncle Raheem. I didn't used to think of owning a business; I only thought of getting a job. And after I bought this business, I couldn't have operated it without Aunty and Dasveer. And if Daljeet hadn't joined us, it would have been impossible for us to grow our sales network. I can go anywhere with him; he gives me confidence. Otherwise, I don't have the guts to start pitching to strangers. I mean, I even took a course in real estate, but I never do any marketing. I just put out a couple of ads in the local newspaper, show listings to the people who come knocking on my door, and so I don't sell more than one or two houses in a year. And Dasveer, she could have found a better job somewhere else after five, six months, but she stayed with us. So please don't think that I'm doing you all a favour. I am doing myself a favour.'

We kept the papers, discussed our sales and planned our strategy for the next three months. I suggested that we should purchase another two desktop computers and that I could give all three of them some basic training in Microsoft Office. They all agreed with me. Keeru said, 'Please make a timetable for the course, and we will follow it.' Then Aunty pleasantly surprised all of us when she brought out samples from her bag and put them on the table. Every item was neatly sketched on a piece of cardboard, the price was listed beside it, and each design had a small piece of the required textile material pinned on it. Tablecloths, drapes, napkins, shopping bags, cushion covers. We were impressed by her painstaking work.

'All these materials are in our stock; we'll make the ones we select during the month of September, then we can start marketing them at the beginning of Christmas season in October,' Aunty declared.

Her idea was excellent. We started figuring out the details. We were all full of energy.

After the meeting, Keeru sat in his car, opened his briefcase, and brought out a joint. 'My lawyer smokes medical marijuana; he rolled one for me. If you don't mind, I'll smoke in the car; otherwise, we can stop at the park.'

I used to smoke occasionally when I was at college in Chandigarh, and later, when I was part of a music band, we all used to smoke together. In Canada, I sneak a smoke with Amarjeet here and there. I smiled at Keeru's politeness.

'You can smoke here,' I told him.

Perhaps I wanted to get a little high myself.

By the time we reached home, I was feeling relaxed.

We were busy working non-stop the next two weeks. Be-Ji was also busy – she was trying to find a wife for Keeru.

Bella would find ads on the internet and read them out to her. Aunty would spend her lunch break inquiring about eligible Muslim girls on her phone. When we got home, we'd see the pictures of the prospective girls. Bella would forward them to Keeru, and to me too.

My Bee-Ji, sitting all the way in Chandigarh, was doing the same thing. As soon as I told her about the sales manager job on the phone – I hadn't even mentioned the partnership yet – she told me that she had picked a girl and was going to make sure I got married next year.

I know that at least Bee-Ji would listen to me. I can't say the same for Bapu-Ji. When I wanted to cut my hair, I first shared my desire with Manpreet and Sukhveer. They were excited for me; they started jumping around when they first heard about it. Sukhveer asked me, 'Where will you go for a haircut?' But before I could say anything, Manpreet responded, 'You better not say anything to Bapu-Ji, or he will cut it all off for you himself – free of charge!' We decided to get Bee-Ji's advice before bringing up anything in front of Bapu-Ji.

When I told Bee-Ji, she couldn't hide her worry. 'Why do you want to cut your hair?' she asked me. 'It will cause a lot of problems.' I told her that I didn't feel the need to advertise my religion on my face. I was a human being before I was a Sikh. She didn't understand me. 'How is it an advertisement?' I tried to explain it to her. 'Some people are human beings; others are Sikh, Hindu and Muslim.

You can see from their physical appearance. People with beards and turbans want to announce they are Sikh. People with shaved heads and dots on their foreheads want to announce they are Hindu. People with beards and mosque caps want to announce they are Muslim. I don't like this kind of thinking.'

Bee-Ji didn't like what I was saying, but she didn't try to stop me. This is the difference between Bee-Ji and Bapu-Ji.

We both got a text from Bella: *Bebe likes her.* There was a picture of the girl with the text.

'What's going on with Bebe?' Keeru sounded annoyed.

'She's pretty,' I said.

'They're all pretty, but they are not going to walk with me,' he responded.

'Why?'

'Daljeet, me and my mom, we are musalli. I think the proper word is Dalit on your side of the border. Our ancestors were Dalit Hindus. They converted to Islam to escape untouchability. But they – we – never actually escaped our caste, not in Islam, not here, not ever.'

'Yes, I know.'

'Oh! Okay.' He laughed, but I could detect a bitterness in his laughter. 'You must have detected my scent. People say that musallis have their own distinct scent and it never goes away.'

'Amarjeet told me.' I didn't have the courage to respond directly.

'Your cousin? Who came with you? I guess he detected the scent? You didn't?'

'Your Pakistani neighbour told Amarjeet. When Amarjeet came to visit me for the first time, he was parking his car in front of the house. Your neighbour came out and introduced himself. He said to Amarjeet, "Oh you have come to visit the musalli house."'

'And you have come to stay at the musalli house.' I could tell that Keeru wasn't going to stop provoking me. He wanted to confront me – but I could also detect his hurt.

'You know, Keeru, I don't think like this.'

'Yes, I know. But I don't understand Amarjeet. He tries to shame you for living with me, but when he sees me, he asks me for a job.'

'He asks me for a job too.'

'Hypocrites are like that. When it comes to their personal interest, they will even call a donkey their father.'

The door opened and Be-Ji walked into the room.

I stood up. 'Sat Sri Akaal, Be-Ji.'

'Keep living, Diljeet. I didn't know you were so smart! Naila says that you have trained them in Micro in one week. She says other people take thousands of dollars and six months to give the same training. I told her, you are a winner of hearts!'

Should I tell her about my name? I was still feeling uneasy about the conversation with Keeru.

'Be-Ji,' I said. 'My name means victorious army.'

'Hmm?' she said in disbelief as she hugged Keeru.

'Yes, Be-Ji, it's pronounced "Dal", not "Dil". Just like tiddi dal: an army of locusts.'

'Ohhhh,' Be-Ji finally understood, 'that's why when you came over the first time, you had such a presence; it seemed like you were not one but many, a whole army, victorious army! Your parents picked a nice name for you.'

Keeru and I looked at each other. We both smiled.

The uneasiness from our conversation started to diminish.

Musalli or no musalli – everyone is a human being.

5

BELLA

I boiled the pasta. It was done, but the lid of the sauce bottle was stuck. What the fuck, I couldn't open it. No one was around to help me. I was to go with Bebe and Aunty at 4 p.m. – we were going to meet a family, a girl, really, to see if she would be a good match for Keeru. I was so excited! Meeting someone to arrange a marriage – I have never done this before! The funny part was that Keeru wasn't even supposed to come with us. First, the mother and sisters go to meet the girl; if we like her, then the boy is allowed to meet her. I didn't approve of this whole process, to be honest, but I was still going. Why? It was a new role for me, a role that has the power to determine two people's lives. I wouldn't decide alone, of course, but I knew Bebe would not agree to anything unless I approved. Never.

What the fuck, someone should have thought of the poor girl too! If someone had come to see me like this, I would have punched all the mothers and sisters and sent them back.

I thwacked the sauce bottle on the counter. Now my blood pressure was rising.

I took out some cold salsa dip from the fridge, poured it on the hot macaroni and started gulping it all down.

It's been three months since I moved in with Bebe (I know, I want to call her Mom, but I also call my mother Mom, so it would get too confusing. In any case, she doesn't feel like a Mom. Keeru calls her Bebe, Daljeet calls her Be-Ji, Uncle calls her Apa Bi, and Aunty calls her Mummy-Ji) and she has never kicked me out of the house, never grumbled, screamed, thrown anything at me, pulled my hair, shoved me.

I am so fucking confused.

I was used to fucking everything up. People always told me I couldn't do anything properly, everyone used to shout at me. Now, everything I do is great, and people praise me all the time. Yesterday, when I got back from the library, I heard Bebe on the phone. She was talking to Aunty Naila, telling her, 'You're right, Bella is smarter than all of us.' But 'all of us' included the genius Mr Keeru, wise Aunty Naila, handsome Mr Daljeet, intellectual Uncle Raheem, and… of course, there was Bebe. I can't find the right word for her. She is like soil itself – or water. Without her, there is no life.

She was at her English class right now. She was so excited to go to class and learn, I felt jealous. I thought, *I should also enrol in some classes at Kwantlen University. Go to class for two days, work for four days.* I interviewed for a job, a cashier at a shop in Strawberry Hill Mall, part-time. Bebe doesn't let me pay rent or pay for groceries. The truth is that I can't pay right now, even if I wanted, but it doesn't feel good. I will feel better once I get a job. Then I can hand Bebe a hundred dollars every week.

I am handling my depression better now. I don't wake up crying or shaking with anger. I can sleep at night, and I don't feel a constant headache. It's still hard for me to go out and meet people, talk to them… I feel anxious. Still, I am not even taking any medicine, and I can feel the difference!

Before, I used to feel odd all the time, on the verge of a panic attack, like something bad was going to happen, like someone was going to blame me for something, like I was going to be punished for a crime I had committed unknowingly. I constantly worried that my elder sisters were going to cheat me again, my mother was going to lecture me again, the people in my class were going to call me 'black beauty' and make fun of me again, my teacher was going to call me an 'idiot' again. I felt like everyone looked down on me, and I always felt hurt about it.

Now, I just feel confused.

As I start to feel better, I think about my mom, and I actually feel bad for her. My dad left her with us three sisters, all alone, and went back to the UK. I don't know how she raised us. I called her the other day, but as soon as she found out that I was living with a Muslim family, she started telling me how they were going to convert me and marry me to an old Muslim man, or how they were going to pimp me out and make money off of me, or how they were going to send me to the Middle East to become a jihadi bride. I told her it was not like that, but she insisted I give her the address so she could send the police to rescue me. I ended the call real quick. That night, I had nightmares again. I woke up screaming. Bebe also woke up and came to check on me. She sat next to me, calmed me down until I went back to sleep. Next day, I heard her talking to Keeru on the phone. 'We have to make space for Bella's bed in the living room. Her stomach is full of air because she is always lying on her side, then she has bad dreams with Draculas all night.'

I wonder: *Why* is she *interested in me?*

My friend, Leslie, whose couch I was crashing on before I came here, and who was always pestering me about money, has a theory. She thinks that these people are so clever that they have turned me into a free servant. I was also afraid of this possibility, to be honest, but I told Leslie that Bebe seems like a simple woman, very innocent. She said that it's always the people who look innocent who are trying to deceive you. A few days after I moved in here, I asked Bebe, 'What should I do?' She didn't understand what I was asking at all. 'What do you mean?' I told her, 'I am staying in your house for free; there must be some work you want me to do for you.' She started thinking. Then she said, 'Bella, I have two little drawers in my room.

Bring one of them here, put it next to the sofa, and put your stuff in it. When you are in the kitchen, don't make a mess, clean after yourself, wash the dishes you use.' I told her, 'I am sorry, these are my responsibilities; I haven't done them, but I will do them from now on. What can I do for you?' She looked irritated, 'You want me to sit down and do nothing, roll around in bed all day until my bones become stiff and useless and I can't sit or stand? No, girl, that kind of life is not for me.' Then I asked, 'If I convert to Islam, you and Keeru will get lots of religious points with your god, no?' She said, 'You ask too many difficult questions, your brain runs too fast (you see, even here, she found a way to compliment me). I don't know about Keeru, maybe he wants these points, but I am half-Christian myself.'

Half-Christian? Why half? Oh, yeah, she is Sikh and also Christian and also Muslim, all at once! I started laughing. 'Bebe, you are crazier than me.' She responded like it was all very simple. 'My Bella, it's all the same thing. God cannot be divided; we can give God a hundred personalities, a thousand names – it all comes down to the same thing.'

So am I half-Hindu and half-Christian?

There are a lot of differences between Hinduism and Christianity. How can it all be the same thing?

Bebe has these brain-damaged ideas, to be honest – everything is the same, we are all angels, don't hurt anyone, kiss-kiss, hug-hug.

What happened to the time?! It was already so late. How would I get ready?! I hadn't even done the laundry. Aunty said it's a traditional family. I think she was just trying to tell me to wear something conservative. I opened all three drawers under my bed. I bought this bed myself, with my own money. I have a babysitting gig, Saturday evenings, $75 for five hours. I used the money I made over two weeks to get this bed. Bebe praised me so much. She did my publicity in front of everyone for days. I found a long, modest purple dress in one of the drawers. It was from Aunty. It looked all right, so I ironed it and quickly got dressed. Make-up didn't take long. I didn't want to go too hard. I knew nobody would appreciate my art there. Just a small, black bindi and some light lipstick.

Bebe got back from her English class. Aunty and Keeru got back from the warehouse. Aunty drove us to the girl's house in Keeru's car. I don't drive often. I'm scared of having a panic attack while I'm driving.

I started feeling anxious as soon as we got to the girl's place. Her mother and sisters kept staring at me, glancing at my bindi. When the girl arrived, she didn't even say hello to me.

Then I started getting angry. My blood pressure started rising, not because of me, but because of the way the girl was treating Bebe. Every time Bebe said something, she pretended like she didn't understand it, snickered to herself and looked at Aunty, then Aunty would translate what Bebe said into Urdu, then she would respond, only to Aunty. She wasn't born here; it's been less than ten years since she came here, but she was acting like she had never heard Punjabi before. Everyone speaks English or Hindi at my house. I learnt Punjabi from the Sikh girls in school. Now I practise it with Bebe. I don't understand everything Bebe says either. The accent also confuses me. But I don't act like this. I ask her politely. I try harder to understand. What was this girl doing?!

I gave Bebe a signal, then I got up, saying I had just remembered an important task. They asked me to sit, offered me some tea, but I told them I had to leave, there was no time. I called a cab and stood outside, waiting.

It was getting hard for me to breathe inside.

The cab arrived instantly. When I got home, I thought I should tell Keeru that the girl was not going to work out, so he wouldn't get his hopes up. I opened the door to his place. And right there, in front of me, Keeru and Daljeet – they were in each other's embrace, kissing. The dim evening light filtering through the window cast them in a soft silhouette. Like the most beautiful painting in the world.

Silent, I turned back.

By the time I got back to Bebe's place, my hands and feet were ice-cold. I was shivering. I turned on the stove and started warming my hands.

They were gay. This was a surprise to me, but the real shock: Why were we looking for a girl?

I started feeling very nervous.

What should I do?

Should I speak with Keeru?

With Bebe?

I am not that close to Aunty or Daljeet. In fact, I am really just close to Bebe. It seems like the easiest thing was to talk to her. I made a hot chocolate for myself. I sat on Bebe's couch and sipped on my hot chocolate.

What if she didn't understand 'gay'? She would get it. I had told her about it before too. I don't know how you say 'gay' in Punjabi. I put the hot chocolate mug in the sink, forgot to wash it and started pacing around the room.

I heard Aunty and Bebe outside. I lay down on the bed and hid myself under the blanket. Bebe came in and saw me, but she didn't disturb me. I could hear them talking outside for a while. Bebe was telling Aunty, 'Bella's eyes are very quick. She took one look at the girl and told me no.' Then Keeru came and said, 'Bebe, stop looking for a girl. I don't want to get married right now.' I listened, hoping he would say something more. He didn't. Then the two lovebirds went to drop Aunty. Bebe came inside and watched TV for a long time. She fidgeted around in the kitchen, ate dinner, then she went to her bedroom.

I was still lying down, still thinking.

I was worried about Bebe, and I was also worried about

Keeru and Daljeet. The one thing that made me a little hopeful about the situation was that I knew Bebe wasn't very religious. Religious people often hate same-sex couples. The second thing that made me hopeful was that Bebe loves Keeru more than anything in the world. He can do whatever he wants, go wherever, come whenever. Bebe is open-minded. Also, everything that had happened at Aunty's house, Bebe asked me about it the next day: 'What was the reason behind your fight with Raheem?' I told her it was about gay rights. Bebe heard what I was saying patiently, even asked questions.

I wondered if one of them was more masculine and the other more feminine. At Bebe's welcome party, when everyone was dancing, Daljeet twisted a scarf tight between his hands like a stick, and Keeru covered his head with Bebe's dupatta. Maybe?

They are a striking couple, to be honest. Daljeet is handsome, pretty face. Keeru isn't handsome, but he is cute. One is fair and one is darker. They look good next to each other. He is a poet, and he is a singer. He is Sikh. The other one, Muslim.

Wow, dude.

If these two found each other, maybe there was hope for me too. Did I want a girl or a boy? I never got the chance to really explore. I dropped out of school in grade ten because of my depression. I can't keep a job, so I don't go to work regularly. I don't have money to go anywhere anyway. Also, I get very anxious when I'm meeting new people.

But now, I finally felt peaceful.

I stayed up the whole night, thinking, *What should I do?*

It's easy to talk to Bebe, but what about Keeru? Didn't he deserve to know that I was telling his mother?

I also haven't told my mom about some things. What if someone else told her when I wasn't ready to discuss those things with her? I haven't told Bebe that I smoke weed or that I am not a virgin. Keeru knows these things. What if he decided to tell Bebe without asking me first?

No, no, I can't out Keeru and Daljeet in front of Bebe.

Uncle Raheem is obviously homophobic. I wore my rainbow top to their house. Aunty liked it; I told her I bought it at the Pride Festival at Surrey Mall. Uncle said it was obscene to have a gay festival at the mall because kids and families are also there. As if gay people were never children themselves, as if they don't have families or kids. Aunty said it is 'unnatural'. How do they know what is natural? I just walked out of there.

I don't want to tell Bebe certain things. Not because I am scared of her, no. But I don't want to shock her either. South Asian women my mother's and Bebe's age think that virginity is very important. Bebe hasn't been here too long. I will tell her soon. She is already dealing with so much culture shock. My clothes, hair, make-up, the way

I talk, my depression, my anxiety. It might be too much for her.

In Keeru's apartment, Daljeet started playing the guitar and singing Keeru's poem, 'Haal'. He had been composing it for many days.

life does not happen again
and again
dance in ecstasy, friend
an ecstatic dance

Keeru came over to say goodnight to Bebe. As he walked out, I heard Bebe tell him, 'Bella has been lying with her head down since yesterday. She doesn't eat, she doesn't drink. I don't know what's happening with her.' Keeru told her, 'Don't worry, I'll take a look.'

He came over and stood next to my bed.

'What's happening, partner?' he asked me.

I looked at him.

I was holding my phone. He was holding his.

I started texting him. He just looked at me. I typed four words: *Do you love Daljeet?* Then I sent them to him.

His phone vibrated. He opened the text, read it. He kept staring at his phone for a while. Then he put it away and walked towards the window. He stood there.

We could both hear Daljeet.

On the edges of
evening clouds
the glimmer of a setting sun
dances in ecstasy over
the flowing glass surface
of the stream

Keeru went outside. He didn't look back at me. I wanted to call him, but I didn't.

He has every right not to give me an answer. Or to give me an answer when he is ready. Or to give me an answer whenever he wants, to be honest.

Daljeet stopped singing.

It was quiet in their place. I could hear the silence.

I stayed in my bed.

After ten minutes, I got a notification. It was a message from Keeru!

One word: *Yes.*

'Yes!' I jumped out of my bed.

I had to tell myself to control my excitement. I wanted to run to their place and hug them both! But I didn't go. I knew this was a delicate time for them. I couldn't share it with Bebe either.

I was restless. What the fuck, I felt so hungry all at once!

Bebe had made some lentils, red and green mixed. I took them out of the fridge and even found two rotis in the basket on the counter.

In the morning, Keeru and Daljeet had left by the time Bebe woke up.

At night, they returned when she was already asleep.

Keeru didn't come over to our place. Daljeet didn't sing.

The next day, Bebe's senses were picking up something. Even Aunty called Bebe to ask if anything was wrong because Keeru was looking sad at the office. Bebe came over to me.

'Bella, may all be well, I am feeling worried.'

'Why?'

'For two, three days, there's no peace at home. Keeru doesn't visit any more, Daljeet doesn't sing any more. You don't look right either. God forbid, is something wrong?'

For the first time in my life, I was completely speechless, to be honest.

Of course, this made Bebe even more worried.

The pressure was getting to me. My anxiety was rising. I got up from my bed.

'Bebe, let's ask Keeru why he is feeling down. Let's go.'

Bebe came with me.

I knocked on Keeru's door – something I had never done before. He called, 'Come in.' We walked inside. Keeru and Daljeet were sitting on opposite corners of the couch. They both stood up when they saw Bebe.

Keeru shot me a look. I shook my head to let him know I hadn't said anything. He relaxed, told Bebe to sit down, asked about tea. Bebe said she wanted to eat something sweet. Keeru brought some sweets on a plate. Bebe prayed for him.

She asked, 'Keeru, my life, keep living, are you feeling well? Are you getting the flu?'

'No, Bebe, no flu. Just feeling… a little off…'

'You guys are working sixteen, seventeen hours every day. Obviously, you are feeling off. Daljeet, son, if your mother found out, she would be unhappy too. Keeru, this is why I tell you, find a wife, you will come home on time—'

'Bebe, please, I don't want to get married.'

'You really don't want to get married?'

Keeru was still thinking when I interrupted. It was all too much for me!

'Bebe,' I said, 'he wants to get married but not to a girl.'

Pin-drop silence.

Keeru and Daljeet turned pale.

I thought, *I made a mistake. What was the point of saying anything?* I was finding it hard to breathe, felt claustrophobic. I wanted to run away, but I couldn't move.

Bebe looked at Keeru and Daljeet, leaned back on the sofa and asked me, 'So then, he wants to marry a boy?'

I stared at Keeru. *Partner, it's your turn to speak.*

Keeru looked at Daljeet for confirmation – he nodded.

'Yes, Bebe.' Keeru finally said it.

He said it – but both their faces turned even paler.

I looked at Bebe. She looked calm. Very strange.

She asked Keeru, 'And this boy, we will have to find him, or…?'

They both blushed.

'No need to find him.' Keeru's eyes sparkled, and a laugh escaped his mouth.

'Then let's eat something sweet to celebrate.' Bebe pulled the plate of sweets closer, put a round, yellow laddu in Keeru's mouth, one in Daljeet's mouth, one in my mouth, and then she ate two laddus all by herself.

Everything had changed in ten minutes!

I felt dazed – I think Keeru and Daljeet must have felt the same way. Like we couldn't wrap our heads around what had just happened. This doesn't happen in our world. Gay people face a lot of opposition; all kinds of terrible things are done to them. So much so that even now, even in this country, their lives can be in danger at any moment.

'Bella, we have to get them engaged this very Sunday. Text Naila and tell her.'

'Be-Ji.' Daljeet spoke up.

'Son?'

'I am in complete agreement with you, hundred per cent, but Be-Ji, all this is happening very fast…'

'Yes, Bebe, I feel like the world is spinning!' Keeru came and stood next to Daljeet.

'Okay, whenever you want, we will do the engagement. But, Keeru, hear me out, I want to celebrate your engagement and your marriage too.' Bebe stood up to leave. As she was walking out, Keeru shouted, 'Long live Bella!'

I ran towards them and hugged them both. Now, I don't have one, but two best friends.

In the evening, Keeru and Daljeet brought some champagne with the groceries. Daljeet said he would cook a yogurt curry, just like his Bee-Ji, and Keeru started preparing some chicken wings and white rice. They both looked fresh in their matching clothes – Daljeet was wearing blue jeans and a white T-shirt; Keeru was wearing white jeans and a blue T-shirt.

'There he comes, my winning heart army!' Bebe called from the bedroom.

Daljeet laughed loudly. He used to laugh before when Bebe called him too, but now, there was an abandon in his laughter. He looked happier than ever before.

In fact, now that we were all together again, we wanted to ask Bebe why she was so calm about the news of her son being gay. Keeru started the conversation. 'Bebe, you are not even educated. How do you understand all these things so well?'

'Look at that. You think anyone learns about these things in school? These are matters of life, of people who live and feel alive.'

'Still, Be-Ji, how did you decide so quickly?' Daljeet asked her.

'It's been three, four months since I have been trying to find a match for him. It wasn't so quick after all.'

'So easily, Bebe,' Keeru said. 'You decided so easily… about us… You accepted us so easily?'

Bebe started thinking. Then she said, 'First thing is that these relationships are not new to me. Keeru, keep living, do you remember Saeen Manka, the Saint of Beads?'

'Yes, I remember him. Chunnu and I would go looking for beads at his and Jhooray Saeen's hut near the graveyard.'

'Manka and Jhoora, God bless them, they have been together for twenty-five, thirty years at this point. And that teacher who lived with her aunt, she wasn't really her aunt, you know. And our Baba Khan—'

'Baba Khan!' Keeru was taken aback. Then he turned to Daljeet. 'Baba Khan was my first crush, but I didn't know it at the time.'

'You didn't tell me before, otherwise, I would've gotten on a plane to Lahore and only returned after defeating Baba Khan in a duel!' Daljeet responded.

They both burst out laughing.

Joy transforms everything. Even their faces looked different, to be honest. I couldn't help but smile looking at them.

'People don't want to admit it, but many of our respected Sufis had the same inclination. Baba Bulleh Shah and Shah Inayat, Shah Hussain and Madhu Lal.'

Bebe took out a few hundred dollars from her pocket and started circling them around their heads to protect and bless them. She handed me a note, so I also circled it around their heads and then put it on the table. Three hundred dollars in total. She told them, 'Take one hundred to the mosque, one hundred to the gurdwara and one hundred to the church. Go together.'

I asked, 'What about the temple?'

'We will send money to the temple when it's your engagement.' She pretended to circle money around my head as she laughed.

I blushed.

'So now you're going to get on my case?' I pretended to be angry.

'Bebe, you should open a marriage bureau; you will be very successful!' Keeru told her.

'Be-Ji, you were saying…' Daljeet brought us back to the topic of our conversation.

'Yeah, you were saying that none of this is a new thing for you,' I reminded her.

'Yes, back home, people must hide from cruel people. Bella told me the other day that here, men who love men are called gay, and the women who want other women are called lesbon.'

'Not lesbon, Bebe, *lesbian*. Lez-bee-en,' I corrected her. Bebe couldn't pronounce it that day either.

'Bee-en. Lez-bee-en.' Bebe got it. 'Bella also told me that gay couples can get married here. They can have kids. I don't know how it happens, but it made me stop worrying. I want my son to have kids.'

'How did you find out about us? Bella told you?' Keeru asked.

'No, no. Bella only said what she said in front of you today. But I could tell, a little bit, that something was going on between you two. The first day, Keeru, God bless you, when I asked for alcohol at the party, and you weren't sure, you didn't ask Raheem or Naila for advice; you looked at Daljeet, and Daljeet gave you permission with one glance. I thought, he must be my son's old and trusted friend. But then I found out you had only met him two days ago. Then you recited your poem, and the way Daljeet admired you, and how happy it made you, his admiration…' Bebe started crying. 'My darling God, you heard me. All I wanted was my son to be happy; I don't want anything else, darling God…'

Keeru and Daljeet hugged Bebe. I joined the hug too. She kept crying. Then she said, 'Bella, you see this? You have two brothers now; don't ever feel helpless again.'

I felt stronger, sturdier – my brothers made me feel powerful.

Brothers can take away your power too. They can hurt their sisters, even kill them. I remembered Qandeel, the internet model, who was killed by her brother.

I saw Keeru and Daljeet serving Bebe dinner in the living room so she wouldn't have to get up. These were not those kinds of brothers. These brothers will stand up for me. That's why I felt powerful.

Before she could start eating, Bebe remembered Aunty Naila. She wanted to give her the good news straightaway.

'Are you crazy?' I asked. 'She thinks this kind of love is unnatural.'

'Nature is everything in our universe, all of it, and there are all kinds of beings in the universe,' Bebe said. 'Bella, she is not stupid like Raheem. Naila is smarter than that. And she cares about Keeru. She will understand.'

'We will see.' I took out my phone and started texting Aunty.

'I don't know how I am going to tell my Bee-Ji,' Daljeet said.

'That sister of mine lives with her husband. Lucky women like her, who get to live with their husbands, don't know much about the world outside of their parents and in-laws since they are not encouraged to step outside. But, son, you also don't have to step outside to know these things. There are people like you in every family, always have been. I am sure she knew about you before you even figured it out yourself.'

'Bebe, since you are answering everyone's questions, I have a question too,' Keeru said.

'And what is that?' Bebe started laughing. She already knew.

'Why did you name me Keeru?'

'Bebe told us that—' I started speaking, but Keeru cut me off.

'Yes, Bella told me, all different kinds of insects, their steadfastness, perseverance. What next...' Keeru looked very serious.

'My darling, what could I give you other than a name? If your father or grandmother were alive, I wouldn't even have had that much. I wanted to give my son a name that was all his own. Every name I knew was related to a religion, a belief. What do weak and poor people have to do with religion? If I had given you a Muslim name, people would have complained that your mother is Christian, and if I had given you a Christian name, people would have complained that your father is Muslim. I wanted to give you a name that wasn't related to any religion. Maybe people don't understand Keeru, maybe they get the wrong idea, but I don't care. I know insects, I know them very well, I hold them in high regard. You just see, you will start to see it too.'

'Okay, Bebe, time to go. We have to pick up Aunty.' I picked up the car keys and started walking.

Bebe followed me.

As soon as we arrived at Aunty's, she got in the back seat of the car, and Bebe announced the news to her. 'Congratulations, Naila! We found a match for Keeru.'

'Really, Mummy-Ji?'

'Yes. Keeru chose himself.'

'Where, who?' Aunty leaned forward in excitement.

'Our – God bless him – Daljeet.'

'Daljeet?' She leaned back.

'He's a handsome kid, hard-working, employed, plays the guitar…'

'You don't have a problem with it, Mummy-Ji?'

'Daughter, why would I have a problem? I am happy that my son's heart is happy. I'm going to leave this world in five, ten years, and I want to leave my son happy, laughing, living his life.'

Aunty was quiet for a minute. Then she congratulated us right then and there. 'Mummy-Ji, many congratulations. Bella, to you too, and to me too.'

'But, Aunty, you thought it was unnatural?'

'Yes, you're right, but these days, I feel as if a lot of my ideas, my beliefs, are not really my own. I think they are my ideas because I am influenced by all the propaganda around me. Now I have a chance to figure out what I really believe, on my own, for myself, so I will try to understand this thing too.'

The next day, I took Bebe to the warehouse for lunch. I drove the car.

The office looked different. With Keeru and Daljeet in the main office, it looked quite posh now. Aunty's cute office was in what used to be the storage room. We distributed sweets in the whole office without giving any reason.

As we were leaving, Bebe said, 'Bella, I forgot to tell you last time, but I want a picture of the front door, where it says my name, "Haleema Bibi Enterprises Limited, Unit 33". Inside, there is my son's name, his full name, "Muhammad Hussain Khan Keeru, President". Now there will be another name next to him, "Sardar Daljeet Singh, President". God has made eleven out of my one.'

Eleven out of one, I didn't know what she meant – Bebe is crazy, I swear – but Bebe read the door correctly, and her prediction proved correct too. Now Keeru and Daljeet's names come together everywhere. Daljeet made songs out of Keeru's 'Kaal' and 'Haal'. Both songs were superhits. They even made music videos for them. Both Keeru and Daljeet were featured in the videos. And me too!

I guess I was superhit too now.

But Keeru and Daljeet didn't come out.

People in the community thought that Keeru wrote the songs for me, and Daljeet sang them for me, lol.

6

AND NOW...

It's been a month since Aunty left Uncle and started living with Bebe. Now she sleeps on Bella's bed, and Bella is back on the sofa. Bebe wants to buy a new bed. She says, in the morning, we can turn it into a divan by changing the cover and tossing some cushions on it.

The day Aunty moved to Bebe's place, Daljeet and I went to meet Uncle Raheem. I told him, 'I am here with you, but I will not tolerate any abuse towards Aunty.' Daljeet supported me and agreed with me. Uncle said he wanted to do the right thing; he was ready to apologize for any past abuse, and he wanted us to bring Aunty back. I told him, 'She's home, she's safe; give her time, and you take some time too.' We started drinking, he started crying. He wept, 'I have no one to call my own, and now I am disabled. What should I do?'

Honestly, I felt a little bad for him. Daljeet made a great suggestion; he said, 'Let's make Uncle our Sales Coordinator. We can give him a company phone, install a sales system on his laptop, he could collect orders over the phone or online without leaving his home. Maybe it will be good for him to stay busy. It would reduce the workload for Aunty and Dasveer too.'

It took us a week to install all the systems and train Uncle. Now, he works from home, 9 a.m. to 3 p.m. He gets a salary, makes commission too.

Aunty Naila has fantastic production and marketing sense. The designs she made for Christmas in September were very popular with our customers. We have now started sending out products for the new year. She is taking a course in graphic design, and she wants to study textile design too. She still doesn't speak or meet with Uncle, but she's feeling better, she doesn't talk about him and, for now, she's given up the idea of filing for divorce. Daljeet thinks that she's so occupied with her work and part-time study that she doesn't have time to keep revisiting her past.

It's good to be a little distracted, I think, get a little break.

No talk of going to college yet, but Bella did something amazing. When she and Bebe accepted me and Daljeet as a couple, that weekend, we went camping at Golden Ears Park to celebrate. There, Daljeet finished composing 'Haal'. When we returned, we presented it in a gathering at the Seniors Centre. Daljeet sang it beautifully. Everyone loved it, and there were lots of requests for more. Bella recorded it all on her phone, and later, edited it to make a music video. She uploaded it on YouTube. I have to say, it has become very popular! After that, Bella got the chance to work on Punjabi TV channels. Now she is an anchor of a youth programme on TV, where she hosts discussions on social issues every Tuesday.

We got offers from different music companies to make an album, but we are not in a rush. When we have enough songs, we will contact them.

Bebe is still doing her English course. Now she can read books meant for children in Grade 2. She has also started learning how to read Punjabi – just because she wants to read my poems. Daljeet transcribes my poems in Gurmukhi, so she has started learning the Gurmukhi script too. This is her first winter here, but she says she doesn't feel cold at all.

How can she feel cold? She herself is the warmth.

It's now the beginning of December. Bebe arrived at the end of May. In six months, my life has changed – it feels full now. I met Daljeet, Bebe settled with me, Bella entered our lives. Aunty and Uncle were already here. Now my life has my poems, Daljeet's songs, the fruits of each season, a roof over my head, food to eat.

If one doesn't feel fulfilled, it doesn't matter how many dollars you have, life doesn't feel complete.

I never thought I would find a partner – I found Daljeet. Bella and Bebe accepted us wholeheartedly. I can't believe my luck.

Bella is right; she doesn't think we should tell the whole community right now, at least not till Daljeet's family arrives here. We don't need to tell anyone until then. We are still learning new things about ourselves, finding each other. *Meeni dhaggi naam saeen da andar beh ke cho*: The beloved's name is a short cow; sit inside and milk.

Why did it take us so long to find ourselves?

I didn't want to find the same kind of man inside me that I was taught to hate my whole life. What could be a bigger injustice? I was forced to hate my own reality. I am also learning that the same propaganda machinery that wanted me to hate the love inside me also wanted me to believe that my whole caste is wretched, low, inferior; the same machinery says that some beliefs are inferior, some human beings are inferior. Daljeet and I grew up hearing and believing these things. It will take us time to free ourselves from them.

Depression, disorientation, anxiety. When the alien inside me overwhelms me, my relationship with everything and everyone breaks down. The street I am walking on suddenly becomes any street. My door is suddenly any door. My office is suddenly anyone's office, situated anywhere. Even if this condition only lasts for a moment, I must recompose and reorient myself all over again. This is still not easy for me.

We are lucky to be surrounded by warmth. Bebe, Bella, Aunty, Uncle – they all care for us, respect us, love us. Daljeet and I want everyone to feel this warmth, for the world to somehow turn and transform, become a safe place for everyone to meet themselves.

The new decade is here, a new beginning, and that is what we will do.

AUTHOR'S ACKNOWLEDGEMENTS

I began writing a novel with a protagonist called Keeru in 1975 in Lahore that accompanied me to the UK in 1976, and it was left behind when I moved back to Pakistan in 1978. My sincerest gratitude to Tim Hume and Caroline Hume for keeping the manuscript safe with them in Brighton until 2014 when Tim sent it to me in Vancouver. That partial manuscript became Keeru's backstory, and this novella would not have been possible without it.